Did I Say That Out Loud?

Best Regards—

Kelly Harmes

DID I SAY THAT OUT LOUD?

Conversations About Life

By Kelly McDermott Harman

wegost
press

Author's Note: The events described in this book are 87% true.
The other 13% can be attributed to my Irish heritage. Certain
characters have been given fictitious names. However, most of
you will know who you are.

Interior Design by Otto Dimitrijevics

Book Cover Design by Monkey C Media

Quantity sales: Special discounts are available on quantity
purchases. For details, contact the author at kellyoutloud@
gmail.com.

Did I Say That Out Loud?/ Kelly Harman. — 1st ed.

ISBN 978-0-9892405-0-5

Dedication

For Bob, who believed in me long before I believed in myself.

Acknowledgements

I love this part of the book because I get to thank everyone who helped make my dream a reality. This part of the book also terrifies me, because I am worried that I will leave someone off this list, thus ruining a life-long friendship. However, I am going to do my best to get it right.

I would first like to thank the many friends and family members who, over the years, have encouraged me to write this book. You have no idea how much your notes and comments have meant to me. In particular I'd like to thank Pat Maccini. You gave me the plaque engraved with the words "Did I say that out loud?" that inspired both the name of my blog and this book. As for the rest of my wonderful friends, many of you will recognize yourselves in various stories. How lucky am I, to be surrounded by such witty people so willing to be fodder for my writing?

I would like to thank Ellen Martin, my "bestest" best friend, for scheduling my first reading before I had committed to actually writing the book. She believed that having a deadline would be a good way to set a fire under my butt, and it worked. Ellen, for reasons far beyond setting deadlines, I love you. Thank you for being part of my life and for your gift of friendship.

I would like to thank Christie Rolon, Beth Pierce, Liddy Heneghan, Len Leatherwood, Katherine Gotthardt, and Laura Biondi. Because of their invaluable feedback and editing services, I appear far wittier and grammatically correct than I ever thought possible.

If you make it through to the end of this book, you'll realize how fortunate I am to be part of a pretty incredible family. I owe it all to my parents, John and Patsy McDermott, who chose not to abandon me during my horrible teen years but to stick by me through temper tantrums, slamming doors, and hundreds of dramatic exits. Quite frankly, I was exhausting.

I also owe a debt of gratitude to my sister, Lesley, and my brother, Daniel, who not only managed to survive, but thrive while living under my thumb. They have both grown into incredibly interesting and successful adults who fill my life with laughter and happiness. Most importantly, they have forgiven me for every mean thing I ever did to them in their youth. Well, almost. There is still the one incident that can never be discussed.

Finally, I want to thank my husband, Bob, and my sons, Gary, Mark and Daniel. The four of you are my world. Even when I am yelling at you, I am loving you on the inside.

If you ask me what I came to do in this world, I, an artist, will answer you: I am here to live out loud.

— Émile Zola

Table of Contents

Part One

The Unexpected

Wax Kit for Sale

I just tried to give myself a bikini wax. I am now covered in pink sticky goo. It is everywhere — my desk, my hands, the microwave, my underwear, my leg, my pants, the garbage can, my computer keyboard, and quite possibly, my cat, Sadie. How did I get here, you ask? It all started with the question, "How hard can it be?"

It occurred to me about a week ago that my wedding anniversary was right around the corner. For reasons that I now cannot fathom, I decided to purchase a "do-it-yourself" home wax kit. I came home, put the box in a bathroom drawer and promptly forgot about it.

This morning I came downstairs to find a lovely anniversary card waiting for me on the kitchen table from my husband, Bob. He is very lucky that he has Hallmark to tell me how much he loves me. I gave him a big hug as he left for work and settled down in my home office for a day full of conference calls, webinar training sessions, and project management.

At about 10:45 I remembered my wax kit. I wasn't sure how long it would take to give myself a bikini wax, and I had a pretty full schedule. I decided to kill two birds with one stone and give myself the wax job while I was attending the 11:00 webinar session. After all, it was just watching computer slides while I listened to the presenter on my telephone. I could push the speakerphone button and put the phone on mute. In addition, the instructions said to melt the wax in the microwave, which was in the kitchen next to my office, so this could not be any more convenient!

Carefully following the directions on the box, I heated the wax in the microwave. While stirring the pot, I accidentally got some of the hot-pink wax on the handle of the black microwave. I carried the heated wax, along with all the accoutrements, to my office. I dialed into the conference call and connected to the presentation via my computer. Once I confirmed I was connected to the webinar, I muted my phone and dropped my pants down to my knees. I left on my underwear. After all, this was a bikini wax. The instructions said to take the wooden applicator and smear the pink wax onto the area to be treated. As I started smearing the goo onto my right thigh, I remembered that the glass windows on either side of my front door provided a clear view into my office. I sent up a mental prayer asking that no one come to the front door until this process was completed.

Those wooden applicators are kind of tricky to hold, and I got some wax on my desk while I was trying to apply it to my thigh. I then proceeded to get wax on my pants, my chair, and my underwear. My cat, Sadie, decided to inspect what I was doing and got too close to the applicator. I yelled at her and tried pushing her away, which resulted in my having to pick cat fur off the applicator. I am pretty sure her nose was hot pink when she ran back into the kitchen.

The process so far had taken so long that my computer monitor had gone to sleep, and I could no longer see the slides for the presentation. Not that it mattered, because I had stopped listening to the presenter about the same time Sadie jumped on my lap. But I swear I thought my hand was clean when I touched the keyboard to wake up the monitor.

Step three in the instructions said to carefully place a strip of muslin over the wax on my leg. Smoothing the cloth into place, I double-checked the telephone to make sure I was still muted. I then quickly ripped off the strip of muslin and screamed "GOD BLESS AMERICA!" at the top of my lungs.

At this precise moment the UPS man dropped a package off at my front door and rang the doorbell. By the speed in which he returned to his delivery truck, I suspect he heard me scream, looked through the window, and saw a maniacal woman with her head thrown back in agony, sitting in a chair with her pants down around her ankles and hot pink blobs flying everywhere and decided that a quick retreat was the wisest course of action.

I threw the strip of muslin into the trashcan under my desk, where it now remains, stuck on the side of the barrel. I tried taking off the remaining wax with the remover in the box because there is no frigging way I am doing that again. Ever. For the record, the wax remover is worthless.

I then applied the "soothing lotion" that came in the kit, but it is tinted for what appears to be an Asian woman suffering from jaundice. My right thigh is now pale white, hot pink and taupe-yellow, depending on where you look. I also have a small bruise, and how the hell that got there, I have no idea. I still have splotches of hair in a few places, and in others, I am missing a layer of skin.

I have decided to shave the left side.

Anyone who would like to have a barely used GiGi Crème Wax Microwave Formula Hair Removal System Specially Formulated for Sensitive Skin, you know where to reach me.

Potty Training is Not for Sissies

"Where is her diaper bag?" I asked my son as he dropped off my three-year-old granddaughter.

"Amie is potty trained; she doesn't need a diaper bag anymore," he replied.

Amie promptly pulled down her pants to show me her Big Girl Panties.

"Wow, that was fast," I said. Then I turned to Amie. "Let's go swimming!"

The two of us went to the local community center and spent a lovely hour swimming in the kiddie pool. I put Amie in swimming diapers just to be on the safe side. I don't really care if she pees in the pool, as everyone knows the liquid in a kiddie pool is half chlorine and half urine anyway. But I did not want any other type of accidents to happen in that water.

After our swim, we went into the locker room to change. While I dressed, a naked Amie played peek-a-boo by backing into an empty locker and pretending to shut the door. All the ladies in the locker room were smiling at her cuteness. That is, until she stood up in front of the locker and began to pee on the floor.

"I'm peeing," said Amie.

"I see," I replied, dropping a towel on the floor and plopping her on top of it. "If you're going to pee, then pee on the towel."

"Okay."

Suddenly Amie began to squat down on the towel. "I have to poop," she said.

"NO!" I yelled. "No pooping on the towel!"

I grabbed Amie's naked body and ran to the toilets. "Pooping toddler, out of my way!" I yelled to the women.

I managed to get Amie onto the toilet just in time. Back at the lockers, we both finished getting dressed. I began to wonder about her status as a potty-trained toddler.

As I bent down to tie my shoe, a familiar odor wafted up from where Amie was sitting. "Oh, please don't have pooped again," I prayed silently. Carefully, I snuck a peek into the back of her pants, only to be greeted by a sea of brown sludge slowly creeping up the back of her Big Girl Panties and down the sides. Amie looked at me. "I pooped again," she announced.

No kidding. Grabbing Amie once again, and holding her as far away from me as possible, I ran back into the bathroom stall. The entire locker room reeked of poop. Nobody in the room was thinking Amie was cute any longer. In fact, several people were coughing.

Once in the extremely small stall, I tried to figure out how I'd handle the tsunami of poop surging from her body. "JUST STAND THERE AND DON'T MOVE," I commanded. I had to leave the stall to go wet some paper towels to help with the cleanup because, of course, I did not have a diaper bag. Arriving back into the bathroom stall, I was greeted with a world of smeared poop. It was all over the toilet, the walls, the floor, the toilet paper dispenser, and my granddaughter.

"Oh, Jesus," I said.

"Oh, Jesus," replied Amie, as she wiped her dirty fingers onto her fat belly.

About 100 paper towels later I had Amie in some semblance of cleanliness. I threw away her undies along with the paper towels, and had yet to put her back into her clothes.

"I thought you were potty trained," I told her.

"I am," she said proudly, standing there naked in front of me with her potbelly sticking out and her chubby thighs quivering with pride.

Who am I to argue? I gave her a hug. "Let's go to McDonald's on the way home."

Great Balls of Fire

If you've been married for longer than six-and-a-half minutes, you've had a fight with your spouse that seemed extremely horrible at the time, but six-and-a-half hours later you couldn't even remember why you were angry. This was the case with my husband, Bob, and me a while ago. He had behaved very badly, and I was furious. I cannot remember why I was so mad at him, but if I could remember and I told you what he'd done, you would be shocked and appalled. It was late in the afternoon, and I was sitting in my chair watching him walk upstairs while I silently fumed. "I don't even know why I am married to him," I thought. I also thought of a few other things that I choose not to write down because if my children read them, they would suffer irreparable damage.

About 20 minutes later, after I'd finished mentally decorating the new condo I was going to move into, Bob came downstairs and took my hand. "Come with me," he said. "As an apology, I've drawn you a bath."

Shocked to silence, I let him lead me upstairs into the master bathroom. Our whirlpool tub was full of bubbles. Candles surrounded the tub, providing a soft glow in the room. On the edge of the bath sat a glass of cold, white wine and two squares of dark chocolate. I was in heaven. Bob kissed me and said, "I'll be downstairs when you're done. Just relax and enjoy yourself."

It took me about four seconds to get undressed and into the bath. "Maybe I won't divorce him after all," I thought.

Needless to say, Bob was somewhat surprised when I appeared in the family room in my bathrobe about eight minutes later. "I thought you'd be longer," he said as his eyes went from the football game on the TV, back to me, and then back to the game.

"Well, Bob, I thought so too. And I need to know that some day in the future, you will do this for me again. As for tonight, I have to tell you that everything was perfect, just perfect, right up until the cat caught on fire."

Yes, you read that right. Lying in the tub with bubbles all around me and chocolate on my tongue, I saw my cat walking on the edge of the bathtub. In a daze of relaxation, my eyes began to drift closed again as I murmured, "Oh, hello, Sadie." Suddenly, I heard a panicky meow. The air filled with the smell of burning fur.

"What the...," I whipped around to see Sadie standing there with smoke coming from her belly. I jumped up in the tub, grabbed the cat and started rubbing her stomach to put out the fire. Being a thankful cat, Sadie then leaped from my arms, leaving several scratches on my naked body. After rinsing myself off, the mood was rather dampened and I didn't really feel like sitting anymore in a tub with floating cat hair and ashes. Besides, I'd already eaten the chocolate.

On the plus side, now when Bob or I have a really bad day, we always start the story with, "Everything was going great until the cat caught on fire...."

Going Around in Circles

"Hello. I'd like to find out how many miles I need for a round trip, business class ticket to Tanzania."

"Well, according to your account,   you   only   have 4,443 miles."

"Yes, I know, but I have big plans. I am just looking for the number."

"When would you be leaving?"

"In September, 2012."

"I'm sorry, but we don't book flights that far out. You have to be within 331 days."

"Look, I'm just asking for the number of miles. Let's pretend I'm leaving in February instead. How many miles to get to Tanzania in February?"

"What days in February?"

"It really doesn't matter! Just pick the first Monday in February and bring me back three weeks later."

"Hmm, I'm afraid there are no more mileage seats available for the month of February."

"I must not be explaining this properly. I don't want to go to Tanzania in February. I just want to know how many MILES I need to get a free business class ticket, regardless of which month. I randomly picked February. Let's try March or April!"

"Ma'am, I would need to know which dates you want to travel before I can help you. And you only have 4,443 miles in your account. I can assure you that you'll need quite a bit more miles for a trip like that."

"Listen to me. Have you ever had a really big, fat, hairy goal? Have you??"

"Ma'am, I'm not sure what this has to do with your mileage account."

"It has EVERYTHING to do with my mileage account. I have a big, fat, hairy goal. I am going to climb Mt. Kilimanjaro for my 50th birthday. I have to break this down into smaller steps. I have no intention of flying for 24 hours in coach. So I need to know how many miles I need to either upgrade or outright purchase a ticket to Tanzania. All I'm looking for is a number. I swear to God I won't hold you to it. I just have to know what I'm working towards. Then I'm going to charge the shit out of the mileage card. Trust me, I'll get the miles. I just need to know how many. Please, do you understand what I'm trying to do now?"

"Oh my. That is quite a goal. Do you climb mountains often?"

"Uh, no. I have never climbed a mountain. That would be the big, fat, hairy part of this goal. So, can you see why I need to know the miles required?"

"Oh yes absolutely! Now, which month would you want to travel?"

"..........."

Coupon Queen

I am going to go on record saying that I was extremely sleep deprived one afternoon. That is why I decided to go to Walmart to pick up seven items. Standing in line with 54 people behind me and two people in front of me, after reading People Magazine, US Magazine and the The National Enquirer, it occurred to me that the cashier had the IQ of an ostrich.

The guy in front of me only had seven items as well, but the woman being checked out had about 432 items, and "Rosie" the cashier had a comment for just about every one of them. "Oh my, have you tried this yet? I heard it is wonderful," she said as she swiped a family-size frozen dinner. "Goodness, what a great price," she exclaimed as she pushed a box of tissue past the scanner. When she finally rang up the last six-pack of soda, everyone breathed a sigh of relief. That is, until the shopper pulled out a wad of coupons about an inch thick.

To make matters worse, every other coupon had a problem. Several had to be manually entered using the extremely tiny printed numbers that Rosie peered at through her coke bottle glasses. The store manager was called over — twice — to determine if a certain coupon could be used. I kept wanting to bail out of the line, but at that point, I had so much time invested I wasn't sure I could start all over again. And since I had already read all the gossip magazines, I just got more and more annoyed.

We were down to the last two coupons totaling $1.75. Naturally, the machine kicked back both as invalid. The woman was arguing that she did, too, purchase the items but she was not going to go through all those piles of bags to find them. Rosie decided to err on the side of caution by scrolling back the tape register to look through the 432 items with her coke bottle glasses to find the missing products.

That is when I snapped. Pushing past the guy waiting in front of me, I slapped down a $5 bill. "I'll buy the coupons," I said. I then snatched the coupons off the counter and turned to the woman. "Keep the change." Then I turned to Rosie. "Just ring her out," I hissed.

"I don't think you can do that," said Rosie.

"Oh, yes, she can," said someone in the line behind me. Then he and several other people started clapping. I turned to the guy in front of me. "Don't even think about pulling out a coupon."

"Not a chance." He held up his hands as if to surrender.

When Rosie got to me, she checked me out without a single word. And when I left, she did not tell me to have a nice day.

Looking for a Hero

"Hello, is this Julian Graham?"

"Yes ma'am."

"Julian, my name is Kelly Harman. I found your ad on Craig's list. You do hardscaping and landscaping, correct?"

"Yes ma'am."

"Well, Julian, I'm looking for a hero and I'm hoping that you are the man for the job."

"Uhm, pardon me?"

"Julian, I'm in trouble. I did a home repair project that turned out great. So naturally, I decided I could do anything. Including lay a new brick walkway in front of our house. Unfortunately, it isn't going that well and my husband is furious with me. I need you to rescue me, Julian."

"Heh, heh, heh."

"Julian, this is no laughing matter."

"I'm laughing with you, ma'am, not at you."

"Well, laugh all you want, but I need you to go by my house tonight and meet with my husband. I am out of town and he said he has to interview whoever I find to do the walkway. I need you to go over there and talk about plumb lines and leveling and show him some of your past work. Can you do that?"

"Yes, I can. I can show him all sorts of pictures of work we've done, and we are very good with levels."

"Excellent. I'm going to email you directions to my house. But Julian, there is one more, very important thing I need you to do for me."

"Yes, ma'am?"

"When you get to my house tonight, I don't care how crappy a job you think I have done on that walkway. Your job is to tell my husband that I was THIS CLOSE to getting it right. Can you do that for me, Julian?"

"I've got your back, ma'am."

"Julian, I love you already. Thank you."

"I'm going to wow him with my plumb lines, Ma'am. I'll make you proud."

My Cat's Butt

My cat's butt exploded. I know this because she waited until I woke up to leap into my bed and place her hind end right in front of my face. In the best of circumstances, this is a pretty rough way to wake up. But that morning, it had an entirely new dimension of grossness.

"Oh, my God, wait until you see what's happened to Sadie," I yelled to Bob. A red, oozing mass of skin surrounded the right side of her back end. I really don't want to give you any more details. Let your imagination do the work and think of those movies where aliens start popping out of live human bodies and you'll get the picture.

"What should I do?" I asked.

"Call the vet," Bob suggested helpfully. "I'm not even going to look at her butt." So I called the vet and explained my emergency.

"My cat's butt exploded," I said.

"What do you mean, exactly, when you say 'exploded?'" asked the receptionist.

"Well, she's got this big, oozing red sore on her rear and it looks awful back there."

"Can you tell if it's a cut or a trauma wound?"

"No, I can't tell you anything except it looks painfully disgusting and I need an appointment."

There are few things in life that Sadie hates more than her carrying case. One look at the contraption and she high-tails it under the nearest piece of furniture. So I have to resort to very complicated maneuvers that include covering the case with a blanket, humming a tune, and not making eye contact with Sadie until I've snuck up behind her and wrapped her in a towel to shove her in the tiny door. If I don't do the towel part right, she spreads her legs out wide and holds onto the sides of the door with her claws and then it's a hot mess.

When we arrived at the vet's office, we were whisked into one of the little exam rooms and the doctor came strolling in with his clipboard. He looked like he was twelve.

"So, let's take a look at Sadie," he said cheerfully. Then he grabbed her tail and took a look at the mess back there. "Well, it appears one of her glands got backed up." Then he stood up and asked, "Has she been expressing her glands in her litter box?"

This was his actual question. How would I know what she's doing with her glands in her litter box? I didn't even know she had glands. I just thought she had a butt hole back there. And I can tell you that there is plenty of evidence she's been using THAT in the litter box. However, I didn't want to actually say that to the twelve-year-old doctor because then it might look like I was an Irresponsible Pet Owner.

"I'm not sure," I replied. "I don't watch her in the litter box. It has a roof over it and she goes in there and does her business. Sadie likes a lot of privacy." Meanwhile, Sadie was trying to maintain what dignity she had left while everybody sat around staring at her butt. Eventually she lowered her head into her paws and started making a strange growling sound.

"Well, we're going to have to take care of this little problem and get her on some antibiotics," said the prepubescent vet. "We'll need to help her express her glands and probably shave around the infected area." He said this with a very straight face. Like the "we" in that sentence was going to have anything to do with me.

"Sadie has claws," I mentioned. "I don't think the whole butt shaving thing is going to go over very well."

At this point, I think the doctor realized that I was going to be of absolutely no use to him. "Well, why don't I just take her into the Special Treatment Room," he said. "And I'll have my assistant help me with Sadie."

Excellent idea.

I don't know what they did to Sadie in the Special Treatment Room, but the sounds emanating from it were not unlike Linda Blair during her finest moments in *The Exorcist*. I was actually pretty impressed. Sadie emerged after about 20 minutes with a shaved butt, exhausted and really, really pissed off. I suspect she'll think twice before exposing her butt to anyone for quite a while. The doctor assured me that Sadie would be fine, and he doubted we'd have another "incident" again. Just for fun, I went home and told Bob that we had to take turns applying ointment onto her butt.

Part Two

Life
with
Bob

A Love Letter to My Husband

Dear Bob,

In the chick flicks I watch with my girlfriends, the guy is always doing romantic stuff for the girl. Sending flowers, writing poems, scattering rose petals, and whispering sweet nothings into her ear. Some of my friends will sigh during these parts and wish their husbands were half as romantic. Not me.

Just so you know, I love you because you buy in bulk.

During our 21 years of marriage, I have never had to look for batteries, light bulbs, tissue, toilet paper, paper towels, or stamps. They magically seem to repopulate in our home.

Now you travel to Syracuse every week and live in a hotel Monday through Friday. You refuse to go to Costco on the weekends because that is when people tend to shop with 13 members of their family. All of whom want to stop and sample every tasting station while walking four across down every aisle. I can't say I blame you.

However, as a result of this new lifestyle, I am currently out of light bulbs. I cannot mail anything because I cannot find the stamps, and I do not remember where we keep the extra paper towels. The laundry soap container is empty, so I've worn the same clothes for three days. I used the last garbage bag four days ago, and I keep stuffing trash into the already overflowing container because I don't have time to go to the store.

I have not watched television all week because I cannot find my far-away glasses. I put them somewhere in the house and you are not here to tell me where you saw them. Not that it matters because I still cannot figure out how to use the remote control for the TV.

Apparently the recycle and trash people come on Tuesday, not Wednesday. I learned this the hard way. And, once again, I accidentally left my headlights on overnight, so the car battery is dead. This means I am homebound because I'm afraid to do that spark plug jump start thing with the machine that has the big pincher grabbers that you do for me every other month or so when this accidentally happens. I know I will get thrown across the garage if I try to do this myself.

I am glad you will be coming home tomorrow because I think Sadie is depressed. I know she is just a cat, but I think she misses you. We have not had bad kitty time for two weeks, and she just mopes around the house. She doesn't even chew my hair any more. You should probably pay extra attention to her this weekend, especially since football season is finally over.

Love,
Kelly

Home Improvement

Dear Bob,

Juan and his three cousins showed up today to paint the family room and office. They are making great progress. Juan noticed all those cracks in the ceiling trim that appeared after the house settled. He said he can fix those and repaint all our trim. I told him that was a great idea. While we were talking, I mentioned that I eventually wanted to paint all the bedrooms. He offered me a great deal so I gave him the "go ahead" to do the extra painting. At lunch time today I offered to have pizza delivered. You could have knocked them all over with a feather. I guess they are not used to having lunch offered by the homeowner. Anyway, we ate four pizzas between the five of us. Painting is hard work.

Love,
Kelly

Dear Bob,

Juan showed up today with four cousins because we have the additional painting and patching to accomplish. They are making great time. Juan noticed that there is a corner in the dining room that is damp. Apparently the gutter over the garage isn't installed properly and water is dripping into the bricks in front of the house. This, in turn, is making a damp spot in the corner of the dining room. Juan can repair the dining room, but he doesn't do gutters. Fortunately, he has a cousin with this skill. Alejandro is coming over this afternoon to look at the gutters. Meanwhile, I told Juan and his cousins I wasn't in the mood for pizza again so we had Chinese delivered.

Love,
Kelly

Wednesday Morning

Dear Bob,

Juan and his five cousins are making fine time painting the house. Alejandro came over late yesterday afternoon, and he explained the problem with our gutters. He can definitely fix this issue, but he is concerned because the water around the gutters and the leaves lying up there may have weakened the roof tiles on the garage. He thinks this needs to be inspected. He said he can't help me, but fortunately he has a cousin that specializes in roofs. Roberto is coming over this afternoon to check it out. The guys are suggesting we do submarine sandwiches today.

Love,
Kelly

P.S. I need to have some electrical work done. Juan's brother-in-law, Enrique, is an electrician so he is coming over tomorrow morning to discuss the project.

Wednesday Afternoon

Dear Bob,

I really didn't appreciate the tone of your last email. Of course I am not going to have the garage roof replaced without discussing it with you first! Juan, Roberto and Alejandro are making sure that we do everything to avoid any roof tile replacement. In fact, Juan and his six cousins have cut a hole into the ceiling of the garage to inspect the roof tile from the inside to see if the water is still leaking through. Also, the painting is coming along very well. The house looks fabulous.

Love,
Kelly

Thursday Morning

Dear Bob,

I have good news and even more good news. After running the hose through the gutter that Alejandro repaired, no additional water came streaming through the ceiling or the bricks, so it appears we solved this problem. This means we don't need a new garage roof after all. Juan, Enrique, Alejandro, Carlos, Roberto, Antonio, Jesus, and Eduardo are just about finished with the house. We're thinking about sushi for lunch as a celebration.

One more thing: Remember when you said having a chandelier in the bathroom was tacky? Well, it actually looks pretty awesome, especially with the new candy apple red paint on the walls and the white trim.

Love,
Kelly

Thursday Afternoon

Dear Bob,

I got your last email. Just for the record, I am not supporting an entire El Salvadorian village. The guys are doing a great job and they know to be very quiet when I'm on the phone for work. They also said my Spanish is coming along extremely well. They are looking forward to meeting you this weekend. Apparently, they also do landscaping (along with a few of their cousins) and are coming over on Saturday so you can walk them through what we want to have done in the back yard.

Love,
Kelly

P.S. When you get home, we need to talk about finishing the basement.

Drama in the ER

I have a theory that the only reason married men stay alive is because their wives force them to eat healthy, exercise, and visit the doctor when something appears to be wrong. A perfect example is my husband, who last year was experiencing difficulty breathing. For two days, Bob walked around complaining that he couldn't draw a full breath of air. I suggested several times that he call our doctor and try to get an appointment. The problem is Bob hates going to the doctor so he kept saying, "Let's wait and see if it goes away."

On the third day, when he still couldn't breathe properly, he admitted that it wasn't going away. Being a man, he got dressed, took public transportation to work in downtown Washington D.C., and then decided to call the doctor's office. At around 10 a.m. he called me on my cell phone, catching me just as I was walking into a meeting.

"I called the doctor," said Bob.

"Well?"

"The nurse said I should go straight to the emergency room because I may be having a heart attack."

"Oh, my God, Bob! You cannot go to the emergency room in D.C. You'll die for sure and I will never be able to find you."

"I know," said Bob. "And I'm afraid to ride home on the metro because last week someone died on the Orange Line and he rode around for eight hours before someone figured out he was dead."

"What are we going to do?" I asked.

"Jim drove into the office today, so he's going to take me home. Can you meet me there in about an hour? Then we'll go to the emergency room together."

This was Bob's secret way of saying there was no way in hell he was going to a hospital without me there to protect him. So I agreed to meet him at home in an hour. With that out of the way, I walked into my meeting and announced I had a hard stop in 30 minutes. In retrospect, I probably had a little trouble balancing my priorities.

One hour later, I pulled into the driveway as Bob was walking into the house. "Let's go," I announced. "If you're having a heart attack, I think you need to be at the ER now."

"Just wait a minute," he replied. "I want to see what our deductible is for the emergency room visit."

"Really, Bob? *Really?*"

"Well, maybe I can figure that out later. But I'm going to go change into sweats. You always have to wait in the emergency room and I want to be comfortable."

Well, he had a point there. Having raised three boys, I have spent the equivalent of three years waiting in emergency rooms. We both changed into sweats and grabbed a couple magazines and a book in case the wait was really, really long. As is pretty obvious by now, neither Bob nor I were too concerned about this whole heart attack thing. Quite frankly, he seemed to be perfectly fine except for the whole breathing issue. About 20 minutes later we strolled into the ER.

"How can I help you?" asked the check-in nurse.

"Well, I'm having trouble taking a deep breath and my doctor said I should come here in case I'm having a heart attack," Bob said.

Meanwhile, I was looking around the room, counting people and trying to calculate how long we'd have to wait. When I turned back to the nurse, she was gone. Just like that – poof, she disappeared. Bob and I were staring at each other, quite bemused, when the nurse and two orderlies came running through the automatic doorway and grabbed Bob. Throwing him into a wheelchair, the nurse started barking orders and using the word "STAT" a lot. Bob looked at me from over his shoulder, wild-eyed with shock. I started running after them as they wheeled him through the mechanical doors. Together we made a rolling blob of people with arms popping out every so often and Bob's head poking up and down like a panicky turtle.

BAM! The orderlies grabbed Bob and slammed him on a gurney. SWISH! The curtain was pulled around us. CRACKLE! The nurse started tearing open plastic sealed tubing and needles. RRRIIIPPP! Another nurse strapped a blood pressure cuff onto Bob's arm. I don't think we'd actually been in the ER more than four minutes at this point.

"What is going on?" I asked.

"Your husband may be having a heart attack," said the nurse. "We need to take his vital signs now!"

Apparently they did not like what they saw. Bob's blood pressure was through the roof and his heart was pounding against his chest. Next came the needle nurse to start an IV. Bob and I were staring at each other in shock. Until that moment, I don't think it had occurred to us that he might actually be having a heart attack. Monitors were wheeled in and little sticky nodes were attached to his chest. Just like in the movies, the screen began to show us the rhythm of Bob's beating heart. And it was beating fast.

A doctor came in to talk to us. Thankfully, he was pretty calm about the whole thing. Sort of like Bob and I were before we came into the emergency room! He suspected that Bob's blood pressure and rapid heartbeat had more to do with the drama of being in the emergency room than an actual heart attack. So he wanted to know how Bob felt about hospitals.

"I don't like hospitals," replied Bob.

"He hates hospitals," I added helpfully.

"Well, I think that he may have pulled a muscle, which is why he can't draw a deep breath," said Dr. Wonderful. "And then he may have had a mild panic attack when he came to the hospital. But I want to monitor him for a little while just to be sure."

I was so thankful that Bob wasn't going to die that I got weak in the knees. "We'll stay as long as you need us to stay," I replied. "I brought books."

Bob and I settled in to wait out his heart monitor. Slowly his blood pressure began to go down. Slowly his heart started to beat more normally. We had both completely forgotten about his inability to breathe deeply. He'd done enough deep breathing during the panic attack to confirm that was no longer an issue.

"Come over here," ordered Bob. He'd been staring at the monitor by his bed, watching the beats of his heart on the screen. "I need you to stand by the edge of the bed."

I walked over to him. "Do you need another pillow or something?" I asked.

"Nope," replied Bob. And then he reached up and grabbed my breasts, one in each hand, all the while keeping his eyes glued to the heart monitor.

"WHAT ARE YOU DOING?" I whispered hysterically. "HAVE YOU LOST YOUR MIND?"

"Be quiet, Kelly," said Bob. "I want to see what happens."

There I stood in the emergency room, with my husband grasping my breasts while he watched the monitor. Clearly we were both past all heart attack concerns. "You're an idiot," I said. "I can't believe that with everything that has happened in the last two hours, all you are worried about is my boobs."

"Men aren't complicated, Kelly. You know that."

He's right. I do know that. They are not that complicated at all. Despite everything we'd just gone through, all Bob wanted to do was play with a new electronic toy and grab some boob. And for the record, the monitor did perk up. It is nice to know that after 21 years together, we've still got a spark. But really, there has to be a better way to test it in the future.

A Collection of Conversations

Botox

"Bob, I'm getting Botox."

"Why?"

"For these two lines between my eyebrows."

"I wouldn't worry about those, you can hardly see them. I'd worry about those lines on your forehead."

....<blink>....

....<blink>....

"Are you trying to figure out how to recover from that last comment, Bob?"

"Yes, I guess I am."

"Bob, there is no recovering."

"I figured."

"But when I get my now greatly expanded series of Botox treatments I'm going to pay from your checkbook."

Mars and Venus

"Bob, I'm so glad you can come to my company Christmas party. The Mohegan Sun is supposed to be a very cool place."

"Yep."

"But since I will have been attending the sales conference for four days prior, I'm going to be exhausted. I have arranged to have a massage at the hotel spa a few hours before the party."

"Ok."

"You can entertain yourself for a couple hours at the casino. Don't gamble away our retirement."

"No problem."

"I've also made an appointment to get my makeup done for the party. I'm tired of trying to figure out how to do that smoky eye makeup thing by myself. Plus I want to try fake eyelashes and the last time I did that on my own I looked like I had two dead spiders on my face."

"Huh."

"Bob, you look confused. What part of this conversation did you not understand?"

"Aren't you going to be spending the entire week at the sales conference with all the people going to the party?"

"Yes."

"They've already seen your face, haven't they?"

"Good grief, what does that mean? Of course they have."

"Well, if they've already seen your face, why do you have to pay someone to put makeup on it? They already know what you look like."

"Okay, Bob. Sharing time is over. You can go watch television now."

Dead Cats

"Kelly, have you ever heard about Schrodinger's cat?

"No, Bob, I haven't. Does Schrodinger work at your office?"

"No. He was a physicist. He theorized that if he put his cat in a box with poison and closed the lid, he wouldn't know if the cat was alive or dead, thus creating a paradox."

"Why didn't he just open the box? And what sort of weirdo poisons his cat just to prove a theory?"

"Kelly, you aren't getting it. It was a theory. He didn't kill his cat. He was a brilliant physicist."

"That is the stupidest thing I've ever heard. It's like asking, 'If a tree falls in the forest, and there is nobody to hear it, does it make a sound?' Who cares?"

"Kelly, you don't understand physics."

"I don't have to understand physics to know that is just dumb. When you leave the house and you're out of my sight, I don't know if you are dead or alive, either. But you don't see anyone calling me a brilliant physicist."

"I'm not going to talk to you about this anymore, Kelly."

"Good. But you better stay away from my damn cat."

Words

"You're typing too loud, Kelly."

"Look, Bob. You're just jealous because I type faster than you can think."

"When I buy that voice recognition software, you are going to be toast."

"No, I'll still beat you, because studies have proven that women say about 20,000 words a day, and men only say about 7,000 words a day."

"Just because you say more words each day doesn't mean you can talk faster."

"Of course it does. I have a lot more practice. I'm going to kick your ass."

"How can you even say 20,000 words a day?"

"How can you not? You'll spend five hours with your friends on the golf course and when you come home, you can't tell me one conversation that you've had with them. That's not normal, Bob."

"Of course its normal. It's a golf game, not a therapy session."

"With women, every event is an opportunity to have a therapy session. Let me show you how it's done. Let's start by talking about our feelings and emotions. Then we can move on to our hopes and dreams. You go first."

"Go back to typing, Kelly. I'm done sharing."

Furniture Shopping

"Bob, I backed into a truck today."

"Good grief, Kelly. How did that happen?"

"I was leaving the furniture store after trying to find a new couch for the family room. I backed into the truck by mistake."

"Don't you have one of those rear-view cameras in the dashboard, where you can see what is behind you?"

"Yes, Bob."

"And two side mirrors, plus a rear view mirror?"

"Bob, is this really relevant? I hit the stupid truck, okay?"

"Why?"

"Why? Why? Because I HATE shopping for furniture. Do you know how many sofa choices there are in the world? Do you know how many stupid upholstery options you have for each one of those stupid sofas? Making the wrong decision is not a cheap mistake with this stuff! It's overwhelming. I was simply overwhelmed. My brain shut down."

"So you rammed a truck instead?"

"No, Bob, I don't go around ramming trucks when I'm stressed. I just didn't see it, that's all."

"What kind of truck did you hit?"

"A Silverado something or other."

"Good grief, Kelly. Do you know how big those trucks are?"

"I'm sorry I even told you."

"Were you hurt?"

"Only my pride when I had to go back into the store and admit that I hit a truck to the thirteen furniture sales-vultures hovering around the front desk. We paged for the driver three times, and I finally left a note under the windshield. Now I'm going to go call our insurance agent and make a full confession."

"Why don't you get that dent on the driver side door fixed while you're at it, along with the scrape on the other side? Maybe you could even get rid of the duct tape you've got holding your side mirror to the car."

"Are you trying to imply something here, Bob?"

"Of course not! Don't be ridiculous."

Barbarella

"Bob, do you remember when I bought my Lexus RS 430 convertible?"

"Kelly, it was a Lexus SC 430, not RS 430."

"Whatever. Do you remember when I bought it?"

"Yes. I also remember that you bought it because I told you not to buy it."

"Don't be bitter, Bob. I was just remembering what it felt like the first time I actually drove that car."

"What did it feel like?"

"Well, since I was used to a Honda Civic with four gerbils under the hood, I couldn't get over the power of the car. When I floored the gas pedal, I felt myself slam back into the leather seat. It was incredible."

"You are never supposed to do that to a new car, Kelly!"

"It didn't break or anything, so don't worry about it. I just remember having the top down and the wind rushing past me and being buried in that soft buttery leather seat. The first thing that came to my head was, 'This must be what it's like to have a penis."

"If that is what you thought, then why did you name her Barbarella?"

"Because I liked the name, Bob."

"I can tell you, owning that car is nothing like having a penis."

"Then what *is* like having a penis?"

"Standing when you pee, Kelly. That is what it's like to have a penis."

"Well, just give me time, I'll figure that one out, too."

Death of a Lobster

"Kelly, why aren't you eating your lobster?"

"I guess I'm just not that hungry."

"Are you kidding? You have been raving about this recipe every since you got it from your friend. You cooked for three hours today. How can you not be hungry?"

"Well, Bob, there was a problem."

"What kind of problem?"

"According to the recipe, I was supposed to put the live lobsters in the freezer. That puts them into a coma. After a while, you take them out of the freezer, slit their throats to kill them, and then you stuff the tails with the crab and shrimp mixture."

"Did they not go into a coma?"

"Oh, no, they went into a coma and then I slit their throats and stuffed them just like I was supposed to. Everything was going fine until I put them into the oven."

"What happened?"

"Well, evidently, finding a lobster's throat is a lot more complicated than I realized. I thought they were dead when I put them in the oven. Unfortunately, I was wrong. The oven woke them from their frozen coma."

"Are you serious?"

"Yes, Bob, I am serious! They started flopping around about 40 seconds after I closed the oven door. They were banging their little claws against the pan. Their little tails were wiggling all over and stuffing was flying everywhere. It was horrible. Can you imagine falling into a nice cozy sleep and waking up in an oven? Then, just when you think it couldn't *possibly* get any worse, you look down and find out that your tail has been stuffed with crab and shrimp?"

"What did you do?"

"What could I do? I went into the bedroom and put a pillow over my head and sang 'La, la, la, la.' It took forever for them to die. Every time I pulled the pillow off my head I would hear them banging in the oven."

"So now you can't eat the lobster?"

"No, Bob. I feel terrible."

"Then can I have your lobster?"

"How can you be so heartless?"

"Look, Kelly, I'm not the one who just murdered two innocent lobsters in the most inhumane way possible. I'm just going to make sure this $65 dinner doesn't go to waste."

Ballroom Dancing

"Kelly! There is no hitting in ballroom dancing!"

"Shut up, Bob. If you would lead, I wouldn't have to hit you!"

"You won't let me lead, Kelly! You keep trying to take over!"

"Oh, great, Bob. Now the instructors are separating us. See what you've done?"

"What I've done? You're the one who hit me, Kelly. They're separating us so you don't embarrass yourself even further."

"Are you kidding me, Bob? They're separating us because you won't lead!"

"Kelly, you need to go dance yourself over to that corner of the room."

"Bob, you need to get hit a few more times. Waltz your way over to my corner."

"Mr. and Mrs. Harman, you're disturbing the class. Can you please waltz yourselves into your own respective corners?"

Romance

"Bob, do you notice anything different about me?"

"I thought we agreed to never talk about your hair."

"I'm not talking about my hair. I'm talking about the twelve pounds I've lost. Didn't you even notice?"

"No I didn't. I never notice stuff like that. Because when I look at you, I still see the girl I met when you were twenty-four. To me you look just the same. Nothing ever changes."

"Bob, I think that is one of the most romantic things you've ever said to me."

Fun With Football

Much to my disappointment, football season is upon us once again. As I write this, my husband is sitting in the living room watching Sunday Night Football. So, here are five things you can do to mess with your husband during football season:

1. Walk past him holding a cordless drill, a hammer, a piece of paper, and a determined expression.

2. Put on a serious face, wait until a critical part of the game, and then sit on the couch next to him and say, "We need to talk about our relationship."

3. Take all your clothes off, stand naked between him and the television and announce, "I'm bored."

4. Download a documentary about the secret life of prostitutes onto your iPad and then watch it while sitting next to your husband. Headphones are optional.

5. Go buy the book *Football for Dummies* and a jersey of the team he hates the most. Sit next to him in the jersey, open up the book, and start asking a lot of questions.

Part Three

Work

Condom Lollipops

I used to work in a male-dominated industry as a sales manager. Five of the six sales reps that reported to me were men, and this led to some very interesting conversations once in awhile. One of my reps was in my office talking about a deal he was trying to close with an association in D.C. dedicated to reducing teen pregnancy.

"They need some references from us," said Tom.

"Who do you have in mind?" I asked.

"Well, one is definitely going to be that association customer of ours, the one that was formed to prevent AIDS," he replied.

"Hmm, that's probably a good idea, they're both in the prevention business."

"Did you know in the lobby of the AIDS prevention association they have bowls full of free condoms?"

"Oh my God, you're kidding! Really?"

"Yes, except they are purple and on a stick. They look like lollipops. I grabbed one while I was there and was trying to unwrap it when I realized what it was, so I just put it in my pocket."

"Good grief, you mean they're condom lollipops?" I asked.

"Yes, I still have it in my desk drawer. Do you want to see it?"

"Tom, I appreciate the offer, but I can't think of one single situation where it would be appropriate for you to show your female boss a purple condom lollipop. Not one."

"Hmm, I guess I see your point."

"But thanks for sharing, Tom."

"No problem Kelly."

Rite of Passage

One of the nice things about managing a lot of men is that sometimes you can mess with them just for the hell of it.

"Kelly, it's Michael."

"What's up?"

"I wanted to tell you I'm working from home today. I have my two daughters this week and there is no school today."

"Okay, that's fine. How are they doing, anyway?"

"Well, they are doing okay, except I think my oldest daughter is about to become a woman."

"What the hell does that mean?"

"You know, she thinks she might be starting her, well, you know...."

"You mean her PERIOD, Michael? Is that the word you're trying to use? Period???"

"Yes, that."

"Why can't you say it?"

"I just can't, I don't know why."

"How about MENSTRUATION? Can you say that?"

"No. My girls think it's funny. I don't know why I can't say it, but I can't."

"Okay, whatever. Is she having cramps? Did you tell you that she has a heavy cramping feeling? Are you prepared for this?"

"No, Kelly, I am not prepared. I really didn't think it would happen on my watch, if you know what I mean."

"Well, at least tell me you've had a conversation with her so she knows what to expect."

"Yes, but now I have to go to the store and you know, well, buy, well, you know..."

"You mean TAMPONS, Michael? Or SANITARY PADS?? Good grief, you can't say that either?"

"Don't give me a hard time about this, Kelly."

"Well, you need to go to the store and get her some supplies. Do not buy tampons. She needs sanitary pads, okay?"

"Okay."

"Now, don't freak out, but you want to get the kind with wings."

"WINGS???"

"Yes Michael, wings. You'll see them in the aisle. There will be lots of boxes and types to choose from. Just make sure you get the ones with wings."

".............."

"Michael, are you there?"

"I think I might call my mom."

"I think that's an excellent idea. Good luck with all of this."

Nothing is Sacred

"So, Michael, how are things going with your daughters?"

"I'm not sure I'm going to survive and they aren't even teenagers yet."

"Yes, raising daughters is not for the weak. But it is important that you keep the lines of communication open, you know?"

"I know, I tried that. I want to make sure they know I'm here for them, especially since their mom and I divorced. So I sat them down and told them they could ask me anything. Anything."

"Lord, that was your first mistake."

"Yes, well, they started whispering to each other and then they left the room."

"I bet I know exactly what happened, Michael."

"What do you think happened?"

"They came down holding your stash of condoms."

"OH MY GOODNESS, that is EXACTLY WHAT HAPPENED!! How did you know?"

"Because nothing is sacred to a young girl, Michael, especially when it comes to her newly single, actively dating father. Nothing. Any illusion you have of privacy needs to be taken off the table right now. You have no privacy. They have gone through every single drawer in every single room in your house, and twice in your bedroom."

"Oh my goodness, what do I do now?"

"Don't kid yourself. If you want to keep anything a secret, you need to lock it up in a strong box and carry the only key on a chain around your neck."

"I never realized girls would be like this."

"Are you kidding me? Wait until they get older, it only gets worse. You're doomed. I have another divorced friend trying to raise his fourteen-year-old daughter and he says it's just like getting a colonoscopy every day."

"I'm not sure I'm going to survive."

"I'm giving it 50/50 at this point. I'll let you know if that changes."

Running Late

"Gail, do you have any questions about this project? I have a flight that leaves in two hours, and I still have a 45-minute drive to the airport. Once I get there, you know there will be some idiot in the security line that thinks the TSA guard screaming, 'Take off your shoes, pull out your liquids and laptops, and remove everything from your pockets' means everyone but him. Then I have to stand in that X-ray machine and hold my stomach in so they think I'm 10 pounds lighter. Thank God they make you raise your arms over your head. My boobs look 20 years younger when I have to do that."

"I'm good, Kelly. I just have a couple more quick questions."

"Fine, but I have to pack up my laptop while you're talking. I CANNOT miss this flight."

"No problem. I just need to know if....."

(This is where my assistant begins to ask approximately 37 questions just to make sure there is nothing overlooked.)

"Oh, my God, you're killing me. I've got to go. I'll have to call you back when I get through security in the airport."

"Okay, fine, Kelly. But don't forget to call me; this is important."

"I won't, I swear. Oh crap, I can't find my car keys."

"Oh, dear."

"Wait, I found them. Shit, where is my power cord!!!!"

"Maybe I should go."

"No, you're the reason I'm running late, dammit. I CANNOT miss this flight. WHERE IS MY CELL PHONE!!!!!!!"

"Uh, Kelly?"

"WHAT WHAT WHAT WHAT!!!!!"

"Aren't you talking to me on your cell phone?"

"Sonofabitch."

"Hee hee."

"If you ever tell anyone about this, I'm going to fire you."

"Snort."

"Sonofabitch."

What I Would Say If I Were the Flight Attendant

In my job I spent a lot of time on airplanes. So much time, in fact, that I had pretty much memorized the safety announcements the flight attendants must recite prior to takeoff. This was probably a waste of time, since I 'd never seen anyone actually pay attention to the announcements. We were all too busy looking at some sort of hand-held electronic device. Not to mention that some of the legally-required jargon is just plain stupid. Demonstrating how to use a seatbelt? Really? No wonder nobody listens.

I think the Airplane Safety Commission (or whatever they are called) should spend a little more time crafting a better, more engaging safety message. However, I know they are very busy keeping tabs on the new Boeing 787 Dreamliner as the manufacturer tries to figure out how to keep the airplane from catching on fire. With this in mind, I have taken the liberty of drafting an alternative, which I am going to put into the mail to the Commission as soon as I can figure out the correct address.

Hello Everyone,

Please take a moment to listen as I explain the safety features of this aircraft. For the guy in 1B who refused to comprehend that a bulkhead seat means everything has to go overhead, and as a result held up boarding for five minutes while he pretended not to speak English, you do not have to listen to a damn thing. We are not going to save you anyway.

Please make sure your seat belt is fastened. I am not going to bother demonstrating how to fasten a seat belt because if you don't know how to do this by now, you have no business being on this airplane and should exit immediately.

Most of you walked by the emergency exits on the way to your seat. Look around and figure out now where you are going to exit if we have to make an emergency landing. I promise you, this is the most important thing I am going to say today, so figure it out now. You folks sitting in rows 25 and higher, just go straight to the exit in the back of the plane because you are never going to get through the passengers in front of you.

If we do have an emergency landing, I would like to ask the little old ladies in seats 9B through 12C, who are clearly traveling together because each of you boarded with three shopping bags apiece plus your handbags, to just stay seated. You are old, you move too slowly and you will just get in the way. When the rest of the airplane is empty, you can exit. I won't even bother asking you to leave your shopping bags behind.

Your seat cushion is a flotation device. In the unlikely event we crash into water and do not sink like a rock wrapped in chain mail, grab the seat cushion on your way out of the plane. This means you will not have room to carry your laptop, purse, or carry-on bag. You will be holding onto that cushion for dear life. So I hope you backed up your hard drive before you left the house this morning. If not, then shame on you.

I am now specifically talking to the two men who were originally in seats 2C and 3A and whom we relocated to the back of the plane for weight distribution purposes. Each of you will need to grab two cushions apiece. I would also recommend you both explore the P90-X exercise video series at some point in the near future. Your seat belt buckles are not supposed to disappear into your belly.

Unless you have been in a coma for the past 10 years, you know that you cannot smoke on U.S. flights. The bathrooms have been equipped with smoke detectors. If you try to smoke during this 60-minute flight, I will personally grab you out of the lavatory and make you eat that cigarette. I will then fine your ass $10,000.

If we lose air pressure, oxygen masks will drop out from above your seat. If this happens, do not panic. If you are traveling with children, be sure and put your own oxygen mask on first before helping your child. If you are traveling with more than one child, well, it looks like you're going to have to make a couple of tough decisions now, aren't you? To the lady in seat 14A traveling with "Little Miss Attitude," I suggest you leave that teenager to figure it out on her own. At that age, they are too mean to die anyway.

The cabin doors are now closed. That means you have to turn off all electronic devices. Do not make me call you out. Hey, you. Yes, I'm talking to you, the redhead in seat 15D. Shut that laptop right now. DO NOT make me use my Mom voice.

We will not be passing out any amenities during this flight because we are bankrupt. You should have packed your own snack. If you need me for anything, you can hit the call button above your head. Only hit it once, I am not deaf. If you keep hitting it, I am going to slap you upside your head when I get to your seat.

Once we are airborne the Captain will come on the speaker to give you more information about your flight. He will sound like a mutant ninja turtle talking through a mouthful of marbles. You will not understand a single word he says so do not bother listening.

Now please sit back and enjoy your flight.

Part Four

Cry
Like a Baby

Cry Like a Baby

"I'm going to cry like a baby," I told the nurse. "I just want you to be prepared."

"Don't worry, you're only going to feel a slight pinch," she replied.

Then she pulled out a needle about a foot long and smiled. I started crying.

I wish I could say this was a bad dream. But this was my day. Since July I'd had a small, tiny, itsy bitsy little place on the side of my nose that had been bleeding, scabbing over, and then bleeding again. Since that is obviously not normal, I finally went to visit my doctor in September. "It may be some form of skin cancer," he said. "Let's try to get you into a dermatologist right away." I think it takes practice to be able to say stuff like that calmly. So I practiced saying, "I may have a form of skin cancer," several times before calling my mother.

Let me tell you about dermatologists. First of all, it takes forever to get an appointment with one of them. They are all booked up at least three to four months in advance. My sister, the nurse, said it is because dermatology is one of the least profitable careers for a doctor. And yet they still have to go through as many years of training as any other practice and take on just as much medical school debt. So not a lot of people pick this line of work. This explains the scarcity of dermatologists and the long wait to get an appointment. It also explains why I'm already questioning the wisdom of anyone who would select this line of work.

I finally got in to see Dr. C. My "hot spot" on the side of my nose was still bleeding. "It's just a little thing," I said. "I'm sure it's nothing and I'm over-reacting." I was feeling very protective of my nose, but according to

Dr. C, it looked suspicious and he wanted to conduct a biopsy, which is another very scary word that requires practice when using it in a sentence that refers to yourself.

"It will be a small scraping of the side of your nose," he explained. "We'll send it to the lab and know in less than 10 days if it is Basel Cell Carcinoma." And that is how I found myself staring at a foot long needle, crying like a baby.

To be honest, while the needle did sting at the beginning, after 15 seconds the numbing agent went to work and it was much less painful. And there is a possibility that the needle was only about half a foot long and I was exaggerating just a little bit. Also, I will admit there was a part of my brain that kept telling me this was good practice to prepare me for Restylane® shots, which my girlfriends have assured me hurt like hell but are totally worth it and completely fill in those facial wrinkles.

When everyone was sure my nose was completely numb by poking it extensively with yet another very sharp needle, the doctor went to work. For all the drama, the actual biopsy took about four seconds. He just scraped a little divot in the side of my nose. The nurse, who by this time had realized I wasn't joking about the baby thing, held my hand through the entire procedure. I was told that the results would come back in about ten days and I'd know for sure if the cells are cancerous. And even if the test was positive, this was a "good" type of cancer, although that was a completely moronic way of referring to any type of cancer.

As the nurse was cleaning up my nose and applying a bandage, she assured me that she'd seen much worse behavior in the past. I did not bother asking if the other badly behaved patients were over the age of six.

Thinking Positive

I got a call from my dermatologist's office. Unfortunately, the biopsy I had taken from the side of my nose tested positive for basal cell carcinoma. So on top of everything else in my life, which had been pretty eventful around that time, I had skin cancer. On the plus side, if you're going to get skin cancer, this was the one you wanted. It doesn't spread, it's slow growing and it's easily treated with out-patient surgery. That didn't mean I was in a good mood about it though. It basically sucked. So I emailed Bob and told him the news.

"That sucks," he replied. "Do you want your Christmas present early?"

"Why? Do you think I'm going to die before Christmas?" I wanted to ask. But I did not say this out loud, because I knew he was just trying to be The Sensitive Husband. And he knows how much I love unwrapping presents. So instead I replied, "No, that's okay. If I open my present now, I won't have anything to open Christmas morning and that would make me even sadder."

Every woman reading that last sentence knows that the only correct answer here is, "Oh honey, I'll buy you another present for Christmas, don't worry." Clearly that was what the moment called for. Unfortunately, while Bob was working on being The Sensitive Husband, he was not there yet. He just wrote back, "Ok, I'll see you tonight."

At dinner, we talked about the surgery I was going to have, called Mohs Surgery, because it was invented by a guy named Frederick Mohs. I explained the procedure to Bob over a nice juicy steak.

"They take tiny pieces of tissue off and look at them under a microscope," I said. "They keep taking off little pieces until all the cancerous cells are removed and all that is left are the good cells. Then they sew you back up."

"What if you end up with a big hole in your nose?" asked Bob.

"I don't know, Bob," I replied. "I guess they'll take skin from somewhere else and put it on my nose, probably from my butt or something. And that's just what I need, another dimple on my butt!"

"Yeah," said Bob.

"I can't believe you agreed with that last comment, Bob."

Bob just stared at me. "I didn't mean it that way and you know it. Your butt is fine. I was just trying to be an Empathetic Husband. I'm sorry I agreed with you." Unfortunately, he did not feel sorry enough to volunteer up my Christmas present again.

Happy Gas

The surgeon's office called to begin preparing me for my Mohs surgery. The Very Helpful Assistant wanted to make sure I remembered to get my referral, bring my insurance card and be prepared to spend the entire day at the office for this outpatient surgery. However, I really didn't care about my insurance cards and referrals. I cared about drugs. I wanted to know what the pain level was going to be like during surgery.

"We'll numb your nose using local anesthesia," she replied. "It should not be uncomfortable at all."

Let me translate this secret code that is used by medical practitioners everywhere. This is what she was really saying:

"We are going to take a six-inch-long-needle and shove it into your nose until you scream for mercy. It will be excruciatingly painful and you will probably need to bite down on a bullet. Then, when you think you cannot take it anymore, the doctor will arrive and start slicing skin off the side of your nose like he is making a salami sandwich."

So I asked her if I could possibly get a little help with pain management. "You know, when I go to the dentist they give me happy gas before they give me the Novocain shot. Do you have happy gas? Can I have some happy gas?"

"When you arrive for your surgery, you can certainly discuss your options with the physician," she replied.

"Does this mean you have happy gas and there is a chance I can get it?" I asked. "What if it takes advance preparation? What if I arrive and the doctor says, 'If I'd only known, we'd have prepared the happy gas'."

"Well, Mrs. Harman, you are welcome to schedule a consultation with the doctor before the surgery," she replied. "Would you like an appointment?"

"No, I just want to know if you have happy gas."

"Well, I'm afraid I can't answer that. Would you like to schedule a consultation?"

"Yes, tell the doctor I want a consultation for three minutes on the telephone because all I want to know is if you have happy gas and can I get some."

"Just a moment, Mrs. Harman. I'll be right back with you."

Now you know that as soon as the assistant put me on hold she turned around to her co-workers and announced she had a drug addict on the phone line.

"Hello Mrs. Harman, this is Dave, one of the physician's assistants. Can I help you with something?"

"Yes, Dave, you can. You can tell me if you have happy gas and if I can get some on the day of my surgery before you start shoving needles in my nose."

"Well, I'm afraid we don't carry happy gas here."

"Then what do you do to prepare patients that are big fat babies? Do you have anything for me? I can't even finish sentences right now because I keep thinking about that big needle."

There was a slight pause, where it was clear that David was wondering why he chose this profession in the first place.

"Well, Mrs. Harman, if you come in about 30 minutes before your appointment, we'll be happy to give you a Valium. Have you ever taken Valium before?"

"Only a few times in the 8th grade, but that was when I was going through my bad seed phase. I love it, I'll take it."

"That's great, Mrs. Harman," replied David. "Just be sure to arrive 30 minutes in advance so it can have its full effect before we begin surgery."

So let this be a lesson to you. Never assume that all will be taken care of the morning of the surgery. The fact that the entire surgical office thought that I was a raving drug addict was a small price to pay for a little happy pill. Not as good as happy gas, but I will take what I can get.

Grafts

Bob and I showed up bright and early on the day of my surgery.

"I'm Kelly Harman, and I'm here for my Valium," I said to the nurse.

She just stared at me.

"I'm sorry, I misspoke. I am Kelly Harman and I'm here for my Mohs surgery. David from your office said that if I arrived 30 minutes early I could get some Valium to help with my nerves."

The nurse pulled my chart, gave me my drugs and told me to take a seat. I spent the next 40 minutes mellowing next to Bob. By the time my name was called, I would have gladly offered up any body part they ordered. Valium is a wonderful drug. I know a lot of people that would benefit from a daily dose, and I think anyone who is forced to drive on Interstate 66 in Northern Virginia (judged the worst commuting experience in the U.S.) should be required to take Valium by law.

It did not hurt that my surgeon was cute. Doctor Wonderful patiently explained what was going to happen and I just sort of nodded and smiled and wondered if his butt was as cute as his face. Fortunately, I did not say this out loud. He put his mask on and looked even cuter because all of a sudden you noticed his bright blue eyes and smile crinkles. You know, those crinkles that look great on men but are supposed to be Botoxed out of women? He numbed my nose and started digging and cutting away. I drifted off to my happy place, and after awhile, he announced that he was pretty sure he was finished, but we had to wait for the lab results. I was directed back to the waiting area with a huge temporary bandage on my nose.

"We have to wait for the results," I told Bob.

"You look ridiculous," he said.

"Keep it up, Bob and I'm going to whip off this bandage and make you look at my bloody nose."

That shut him right up. Bob has no stomach for blood or any type of gruesome, gross body problem.

Just about the time both my Valium and the Novocain were wearing off, Doctor Wonderful summoned me back to the surgery room.

"Well, do you have good news for me?"

"Yes, the lab results show we got all of the cancer. Now all we need to do is patch you up. Unfortunately, we're going to have to do a skin graft."

"Why? Can't you just sew up the hole in my nose?"

"No, you have a very large hole in your nose, and we don't have anything to fill it with. You're going to need to have a graft. I'm going to take a small circle of skin from the inside of your ear and sew it on the outside of your nose. It will be fine, really."

I sat there and stared at him for a moment. My happy place seemed very far away. He blinked his big blue eyes back at me.

"I'm going to need some more Valium," I said.

"Yes, I figured you would."

Dr. Maybe-Not-So-Wonderful then asked if I wanted my husband to sit with me during the second part of the surgery.

"Christ, no! He'll keel over at the first sight of blood and you'll have two patients on your hands. But please bring him in here so you can explain what you are doing to me so I don't have to worry about screwing up the explanation."

When Bob came into the surgical room Dr. Getting-Even-Less-Wonderful explained what was going to happen next. When he was finished, Bob stared at him for a minute.

"She's going to need more Valium," he finally said.

"Yes, apparently."

The rest of the surgery was non-eventful, thanks to a very generous serving of Valium and a preponderance of Novocain. I walked out of the office with a large bandage on my nose and another on the side of my ear. Bob was right–I did look ridiculous. What I found fascinating was that the surgeon actually sewed the first layer of bandages onto my nose. I guess it was to make sure everything stayed in place.

After about a week, I returned and had my bandages removed. You can hardly see the circle on the side of my nose and I have the added benefit of being able to tell people that part of my ear is on the side of my nose. It makes for an excellent conversation starter; plus, I now have my grandchildren convinced I can hear through my nose.

Part Five

The Boys

Why I Hate 6th Grade Boys

Many years ago when my sons were in middle school, I worked for a man who was a former litigator. This meant that every time I wanted to ask for permission to do something, I had to prepare as if I were going on trial. Although it sounds like a pain, it actually prepared me quite well for future arguments with everyone from my current boss to my husband.

I was scheduled to meet with him one morning to ask for an increase in my marketing budget. I knew I would need to be in top form. This meant my first concern was what I would wear. Truthfully, it wasn't a big decision since I only owned one power suit. This was back in the days when my children were literally eating us out of house and home. We lived paycheck to paycheck, and I didn't have a lot of discretionary income to spend on fancy clothes. And on that morning, while standing in front of my closet, I remembered that the power suit was at the cleaners. I'd meant to pick it up the previous evening in between shuttling the boys back and forth to football practices (conveniently located on opposite ends of town).

"No worries," I thought to myself. "I'll just pick it up at the cleaners on the way to work." I then put on my pantyhose and bra, donned my trench coat, and went out to the living room to make sure the kids were ready for school. The morning was progressing in its typical fashion, which meant my two younger boys had decided to gang up and annoy their older brother, who outweighed them by about 75 pounds. A very physical fight ensued and I had to jump in the middle to break it up while screaming at everyone like a fishwife. Shoving them all out the door and hollering at them to go to the bus stop, I got in my car and wondered how much trouble I'd get in if I just stopped feeding them for a while.

I was about five minutes from the office when I noticed that my butt felt very slippery. "Why am I so slippery?" I wondered. It took about 15 seconds to realize it was my pantyhose sliding on the acetate lining of the trench coat.

"Sonofabitch," I said out loud. "I forgot the suit."

In my desire to keep at least two of the three boys alive during the fight, (and I really did not care which two) I had forgotten to go by the dry cleaners. As a result, I was now two minutes away from showing up to work with no clothes on. I had no choice but to turn around and go home. I called the office and told them I'd had a flat tire.

If this book writing gig ends up making me famous, I won't have to worry about getting too big for my britches. Bob is always happy to remind me that I am the only person he ever met who accidentally went to work in her underwear. I blame it all on my children.

Why Mothers of Sons
Go to Heaven

"Dr. K, it's Kelly Harman. I need to talk to you about the boys."

"Hello, Mrs. Harman, how can I help you?"

"Quite frankly I think at least one of my three boys has the makings of a serial killer. It could be more than one, I'm not sure. Since you are their pediatrician, I figured I'd better call you for advice."

"That's quite a concern. What are they doing?"

"It's more of a series of events, actually. On Sunday their father opened a beer and poured it into a mug he keeps in the freezer. As he was taking his first sip, something black floated up through the foam. It was a dead cricket. Apparently the boys wanted to see what would happen if they froze the cricket.

"On Monday I came home to find a horrible black slime on my kitchen counters. When I asked the boys what happened, they informed me that if you put BenGay® muscle rub on a cricket, it melts.

"Then today I came home from work and found fifteen dead crickets nailed to our fence, all in a perfect row."

"Well, Mrs. Harman, I can see why this might be a bit upsetting."

"Upsetting? Upsetting?! Of course it's upsetting! I can't swing a dead cat in this house without hitting a cricket that has died some horrible death! My house is a death camp for crickets! I'm sure this is the sign of a budding serial killer."

"I have good news and bad news for you, Mrs. Harman."

"Oh, my God, what is it?"

"The good news is that your boys are fine. As long as they stick to crickets, you have absolutely nothing to worry about; all boys do this. If they move to mammals, then you need to call me."

"Huh. What's the bad news then?"

"Unfortunately, you've got about three more months of cricket season. You may want to establish some ground rules at your house."

"You know, Dr. K, in a sort of weird and sick way, this has been a very reassuring conversation. Thank you."

"My pleasure, Mrs. Harman."

Conversations with Gary

My son Gary and I are only eighteen years apart, so over the years, we've had some pretty interesting conversations. The birth of his daughter, Amelia, in 2008 generated some of the more memorable discussions.

Prenatal Exam

"Mom, it's Gary."

"Hi Gary."

"Geneva and I went to the doctor today for her checkup. The baby is coming along fine."

"That's great. What else did he say?"

"You know Mom, I really can't remember. I'm sitting in the examination room with my wife, and this guy is talking to me with his hand up her private parts. I know I'm supposed to be cool about it, because this is normal, right? But part of me wants to grab him and throw him across the room while I yell, 'Keep your hands out of my wife's vagina!' Do you know what I mean?"

"Well, not exactly, but I guess it is a bit weird to be the dad and watch that."

"Weird is right, Mom."

"If it's any consolation, by the time that baby is born, an entire high school band could march through her vagina and neither of you will care one bit."

Five Months Pregnant

"Gary, why are you so upset? What's wrong?"

"Mom, I don't know what's wrong. Ever since Geneva got pregnant it has been like this. I've gained ten pounds, my hormones are all over the place and I'm an emotional wreck!!!"

"Well honey, having a baby is a big thing, and every father handles it differently. Apparently, you are going to be pregnant right along with Geneva. Don't worry, you'll be fine."

In the Birthing Room

"Gary, the doctor just said that Geneva has to get a C-section. Is now the best time to be reading a book?"

"It's the *What To Expect When You're Expecting* book, Mom. I hadn't exactly read the chapter on C-Sections. So I guess I better brush up now."

Home from the hospital — Five days after the birth

"Mom, its Gary."

"What's wrong? You sound upset."

"I am, Mom! Everyone expects me to know what to do with this baby. Geneva can't get out of the bed and I'm in charge of taking care of Amie. And I DO NOT KNOW WHAT I AM DOING!"

"Honey, I saw you at the hospital. You are wonderful with that baby."

"Mom, I have not slept in four days. The baby won't stop crying. That *What To Expect When You're Expecting* book is fucking worthless. And I am totally clueless about what to do half the time. Why didn't you tell me it would be like this?"

"If I had told you what it was really like to have a baby, you wouldn't have believed me, would you?"

"No, nobody could believe it is really like this."

"Exactly. Being a new parent is like joining a secret club.

All of us parents know what it's really like to have a new baby. But until you have one, you will never believe how horrible those first few weeks really are. You just think, 'Oh, it will be different for me, because my baby won't be that way'."

"You're right; that's what I would have thought."

"Welcome to the club, honey."

Six Days after the Birth

"Mom, I got a call from Mark today. He and Anna want to know how things are going. Since their baby is due any day now, he is pumping me for information."

"Did you tell him about the secret club?"

"Hell no. Let him figure it out himself. He'll never believe me anyway."

Two Weeks into Nursing

"Mom, when you were nursing me did you have dry, cracked nipples?"

"Gary, I am not comfortable discussing my nipples with you. Where is Geneva?"

"Mom, nursing is a perfectly natural thing to do, why are you so uptight?"

"Gary, I do not need a lecture from my son on the naturalness of nursing. Nor do I intend to talk to you about my nipples. It is just weird. Now put your wife on the phone."

"Geneva, my uptight mom wants to talk to you."

Baby Names

"Mom, it's Gary."

"Hi Gary, what's up?"

"Well, believe it or not, Geneva and I were talking about possibly having another baby some day. And if it's a girl, we thought we would name her Cornelia. What do you think about that name?"

"I think it has eight years of therapy written all over it, that's what I think. Where on earth did you even get a name like that?"

"You know that TV show about the fishermen called *The Deadliest Catch?* One of the ships is named *The Cornelia* and I thought it was a nice name."

"Gary, when she hits sixth grade all the boys will call her 'Horny Cornie'. And when someone asks her where she got her name, she'll have to say, 'My parents got the name from *The Deadliest Catch*!!'"

"Huh. I guess I hadn't thought that one through."

"Clearly. Now put your wife on the phone."

Grandpa's Golf Balls

It would appear that Amie has picked up her grandmother's habit of blurting out totally inappropriate statements when least expected. We were on our way out to go shopping when she walked over to a big bucket sitting in the garage.

"Grandma, what are these?"

"Honey, those are Grandpa's practice golf balls. He keeps them in that bucket."

"Why are they different colors?"

"That is so they are easy to find in the grass. Otherwise he loses a lot of balls. What colors do you see there?"

"Blue, orange, and yellow. They're so pretty!"

"Yes, they are, sweetheart. Now let's get in the car, we have to go buy you some clothes."

I then spent two extremely long and painful hours visiting three different stores looking for pants that would (a) fit Amie's long legs and bubble butt and (b) pass the inspection of an extremely opinionated three-and-a-half-year-old.

Upon leaving the store we got into our 87th argument of the afternoon.

"Grandma Kelly, I want to go that way down the mall."

"No, Amie, we have to go this way because Daddy is meeting us at the restaurant for dinner. It's time for you to go home."

"No, Grandma, please! I want to keep playing with you. I don't want to go home."

"Well, Amie, Grandma is old and tired. I need to go home and relax and maybe have a glass of Granny juice. So we need to go find Daddy and have dinner now."

"PLEASE GRANDMA, PLEASE, PLEASE, PLEASE, CAN WE GO TO YOUR HOUSE FIRST?" shouted Amie as we walked through the crowded mall. "I WANT TO PLAY WITH GRANDPA'S BALLS SOME MORE BEFORE WE GO SEE DADDY!!!!!"

At 9:30 that evening, I quietly sat in my home waiting for Child Protection Services to show up at the door. I was sure it was only a matter of time.

Out of the Mouth of Babes

Privacy

"Grandma, I have to poop!"

"Well, Eli, let's go to the bathroom."

"Grandma, you can't stay in here. I need my PRIVACY!!!"

"Okay, I'll turn around."

"NO GRANDMA, I CAN DO THIS MYSELF, I NEED MY PRIVACY. YOU HAVE TO GO OUTSIDE AND SHUT THE DOOR!!"

"Okay, here I go. The door is shut."

"GRANDMA, GRANDMA!"

"What, Eli?"

"You have to stay by the door because when I'm done I need you to WIPE MY BUTT!"

Royalty

Four-year-old grandson Eli: "I am the King!"

Four-year-old granddaughter Amie: "I am the Queen!"

Four-year-old grandson Eli: "I am the mean King, and I have my sword!"

Four-year-old going on twenty-one year-old granddaughter Amie: "Well, I am the Queen and I have my cell phone so I'll call my lawyer!"

Decisions

"Grandma, I just can't decide."

"Eli, listen to me. I realize that being four and having so many choices is tough. But you are going to need to make a decision. Now, I've spread all seven options out in front of you. We've been blocking traffic in this aisle for 30 minutes. You are going to have to suck it up and choose one of these boxes."

"What about this one then?"

"You can only pick from the boxes I laid out on the floor. That box costs $100 and you are not worth that much money yet."

"Okay...."

"Eli, I'm tired of sitting on this floor. My butt is asleep."

"Okay. I HAVE DECIDED! I am picking the Ninjago Fanpyre car."

"Excellent choice, Eli."

"You really think so?"

"Absolutely. You thought it through, weighed all your options, and made the best decision possible. I'm very proud of you."

"I love you Grandma."

"I love you too, Eli."

Why

"Eli, get your hand out of your pants."

"Why?"

"Because it isn't polite to hold onto your wiener when other people can see you."

"Why?"

"It just isn't. You do that when you are alone."

"Okay."

"Eli."

"What, Grandma?"

"Turning your back on me does not constitute being alone."

Blrghf

"Kendall, why do you have your pacifier?"

"Hi, Grandma."

"Kendall, you know you are only supposed to have that at bedtime."

"I love you, Grandma."

"Kendall, give me your pacifier."

"I'm just holding it, Grandma."

"I better not see it in your mouth."

"I'm just holding it, I promise."

"Kendall, why are you hiding behind the curtains?"

"Blrghf glg prbufl."

Busted

Daddy, I have to go potty."

"Okay, we're leaving the park in a minute. Wait until we get back to Grandma's house."

"But I have to go now."

"We'll be home in ten minutes. There are no bathrooms here, Amie."

"Well, Grandma Kelly lets me go outside."

"What?"

"Grandma Kelly lets me pee outside all the time."

"Uh, Mom? Is there something you want to tell me?"

"I'm going to go start the car now."

Love

"Grandma, who is this?"

"He is a stuffed monkey named George. I got him when I was a little girl just like you."

"He's yours?"

"Yes, he is mine. But he is very old, so I keep him in a safe and secret place most of the time."

"He is very worn out, Grandma. Did you hug him too much?"

"No baby, you can't ever hug someone too much. I just loved the stuffing right out of him, that's all."

"Grandma?"

"What?"

"I love the stuffing out of you."

"I love the stuffing out of you too, baby."

Part Six

Friendship

Penis Envy

Every woman needs at least one "official" gay best friend. This is the man who will go shopping with you, give you advice on your hair, listen to you tell every single detail of a story, and basically do everything you secretly want your husband to do, except you are never obligated to offer up sexual favors in return. I encourage all women to develop a friendship with at least one gay guy.

One of the nice things about having a gay best friend is that when you are all teary and emotional because your body has become a haven for hyped up hormones, he won't try to fix your problem or tell you what you're doing wrong. He just commiserates with you, sends you funny emails to cheer you up, and then tells you how happy he is that it's you, not him, with the problem. That is why I found myself weeping on the phone to my GBF (gay best friend) one day.

"I'm just so sad, tired, and exhausted. I can't talk about it," I wept into the phone.

"What can I do?" he asked.

"Oh, nothing," I moaned. "I'm just miserable and if I talk about it, I will keep crying."

"Then email me," he suggested. "Email me right away and tell me everything."

That is another nice thing about GBFs. They want to know all the details. I emailed my very best GBF all my problems which in retrospect, were extremely small, stupid problems made very large and scary because I had enough hormones raging through my body to push four 12-year-old girls through puberty.

The next morning I woke up to find his response in my email box. He had re-written the lyrics to "If you're happy and you know it clap your hands." Instead I was required to sing, "If I'm sad and I know it, clap my hands." I won't go through the rest of the lyrics, but suffice it to say it cheered me up immensely. He also thoughtfully provided a link to an article on WebMD called "Why You Are Not Happy."

So after I sang my Sad Song and finished clapping my hands I clicked on the link to discover why I was not happy. I had just started reading when an advertising banner titled "Most Popular Articles" caught my eye. Number three on the list was "Five Things You Did Not Know About Your Penis." Who needs to know about happy when you can read about penises?

I had just finished the article when Bob came downstairs to pour his first cup of coffee. "Bob, sit down and listen. I need to tell you five things you did not know about your penis."

He looked at me over his reading glasses and took another sip of coffee. I read the entire, extremely enlightening article to Bob. He was not impressed.

"I knew four of those already," he replied. "And if they're going to start writing articles like that, they should write one about vaginas. Except they'd need a lot more space because those things are really complicated."

Which might be true, but I don't care. At least I can't *break* my vagina.

Ophelia

A few years ago, I was able to break away and fly down to Florida to visit an old high school friend. The older I get, the more precious these friendships become. You know, the ones where you have not seen each other in forever, but when you reconnect, you simply pick up the conversation where you both left it last time.

There is another nice thing about having this type of friend — you don't have to worry about what you say in front of them because they have already seen you at your worst, and have still chosen to remain your friend. This came in particularly handy that weekend.

"Holy cow, Ophelia! What the hell did you do to your boobs?"

"Isn't it obvious, Kelly? I got a boob job."

"No shit. They are really something. Why now?"

"I just got tired of having really small boobs so I gave myself a present for my 40th birthday."

"I'll probably stare all weekend. Don't be offended."

Ophelia assured me that she would not take offense and I could stare myself silly for all she cared. Which I did, because I find fake boobs fascinating. They are so perky and bouncy and, well, fake looking. I wonder things about them, like, if your car's airbag deploys and hits you in the chest, will your boobs pop? When you go swimming, will you find yourself floating more easily than before? If you go out dancing right after having them installed, will you find yourself off balance until you get used to the extra weight swishing around?

I've also noticed that for the most part, women with fake big boobs view their breasts a lot differently than those of us who have been stuck with the real thing since puberty.

Women who have actually paid money for those puppies treat them like a favored relative. They put their breasts in fancy lacy bras that push up each globe until they are quivering like gelatin. These women are so delighted with their new friends that they never miss an opportunity to put them out on display, wearing low-cut tops that reveal about seven inches of cleavage.

Those of us who have been hauling around our boobs for a couple of decades are so underwhelmed by the whole thing that all we care about is putting them to work. We wrestle them into submission and then shove them in good, sturdy bras that are built to defy the ravages of time and Mother Nature. Once that is done, we stuff the side corners and center with various and sundry items. I will typically have my cell phone on the left side, my lipgloss in the middle, and a credit card and driver's license on the right side. Sometimes I get a little carried away and put things in there that I forget about later. If you see me trying to get my car out of one of a parking garages, and I'm holding out the bottom elastic of my bra and jumping up and down, you can rest assured that I have not lost my mind — I'm just looking for the damn ticket.

That evening Ophelia and I spent a wonderful few hours catching up on each others' lives. The next morning I was in the kitchen drinking coffee when she stumbled into the room. I probably forgot to mention that Ophelia is six feet tall, with luxurious, thick, wavy blonde hair that falls past her shoulders. She has clear blue eyes and seldom sees the need for makeup because of her wonderful skin. I spent a few moments wishing I were shallow enough to hate her, then jumped back to the more important topic at hand.

"How did you come up with that size?" I asked.

"I took a bunch of socks and went to Victoria's Secret. I kept trying on bras and stuffing them with socks until I got to a size that I liked. Then I checked out the bra and it was a 34D so that's what I went with."

"I guess that's one way of figuring out what size you want."

"Here's what I need to know, Kelly. When I date a new guy and when we get to the part where, well — you know — stuff happens, do you think I should admit they are fake?"

"Ophelia, they just entered the kitchen three minutes before the rest of you. I think he will know."

"Well, I'm not sure. I mean, why admit they are fake unless I have to? The only problem is, I don't know what big boobs feel like. I mean, real boobs. So I don't know if he'll be able to tell the difference."

We stared at each other silently for a moment. She took a sip of coffee. I cleared my throat. "Ophelia, I see where this is going, and I am not comfortable."

"C'mon Kelly, I need to know."

"Ophelia, I cannot believe you are asking to feel my boobs."

"Well, I can't ask anyone else. You're my best friend, now come on! I need to know if I have to tell the guy or not."

"All right, fine. But I have never felt fake boobs, so I get to feel yours, too."

"Okay, that's fair."

"But listen Ophelia, there will be no nipple involvement. Got it?"

"Kelly, don't be an idiot. I am not going to touch your nipples."

"Okay, then fine. I just wanted to set some ground rules."

Standing in the kitchen, we both pulled off our pajama tops. The looks of concentration on our faces were not unlike those of a sixth grader in the middle of her first biology experiment. About 45 seconds later I exclaimed, "Oh, wow, they're really rubbery."

"Well, yours are squishy, Kelly!"

"Ophelia, mine are real. They are supposed to be squishy."

"Damn, this means the guy will be able to tell, huh?"

"Yes, I'm pretty sure he'll be able to tell. They are sort of like really thick balloons filled with water."

"Hmm. Okay. Well, thanks for cooperating."

"Hey, what are friends for if you can't feel their boobs once in a while?"

How I Got Dumped by My Wrong Number

Several years ago I was calling a girlfriend and accidentally transposed the area code. Instead of dialing 301 (Maryland) I dialed 310 (Los Angeles). When a man answered the phone, I realized my mistake.

"I'm sorry," I said. "I've got the wrong number."

"I … am not … a wrong number," he replied.

I didn't quite know what to do about this response. "I meant that I dialed the wrong number, I didn't mean anything else," I said.

"That's okay," he replied. "My name is Steve. I see you're calling from a 703 area code. Are you in Virginia?"

"Well, yes, I am. I'm sorry to have bothered you."

"No, don't hang up yet," he said. "I'm on my way to a job interview. I just found out about it. Right now I sell office supplies and this is a job selling gourmet food to some of the top restaurants in LA. I'm nervous."

I have to admit, I was a little bit charmed. "Well, Steve, I wish you luck with your job interview. It sounds like a very interesting opportunity."

"Oh, it's very interesting!" he said, and then proceeded to tell me all about the job opportunity. I finally had to interrupt and say, "Steve, this has been great, but I really need to hang up now and call the person I was trying to reach in the first place."

"Oh, that's all right," he said. "It was nice talking to you. Wish me luck on my interview!"

"Good luck," I replied, and then hung up the phone and went back to work. Several hours later, while focusing on a large project, I answered my phone.

"This is Kelly," I said.

"Is this Susan?" asked the caller.

"No, I'm sorry you have the wrong number."

"Kelly, my dear, dear Kelly. You are not a wrong number," said the caller.

"Steve, is that you?"

"Yep."

"Steve! Wrong numbers are not supposed to call you back."

"Well, I wanted to tell you how my interview went. I think I'm going to get the job!"

And thus began my relationship with my wrong number. Every so often Steve would call me to talk about his day (he did get the job) and ask me how I was doing. This went on for over a year. I never knew when he would call, and we never talked for very long. He just seemed to enjoy keeping me updated on his life. I would always work in a brief comment about my husband or my kids, so he would know that I was married and very unavailable. But that really wasn't the nature of the conversations we had; he seemed more interested in treating me as a sounding board for his ideas.

Then one day he called and I was working on a proposal, so I didn't have any time to talk. This seemed to upset him and he hung up a bit miffed. He called the next day and his tone was very accusatory.

"I really wanted to talk to you yesterday, Kelly," he said. "I am thinking about quitting my job and wanted your advice."

"Well, Steve, I was very busy and couldn't talk. And quite frankly, I think you'd be better off talking about this with a friend or colleague, not me."

"Kelly, I thought you were a friend."

"Steve, I don't know you well enough to give that sort of advice."

"So you don't want to help me?"

"It isn't a matter of not wanting to help. It is a matter of not being in a position to give you relevant advice. I don't know you, Steve."

"Kelly, you really aren't the person I thought you were."

"Steve, I'm NO PERSON you thought I was, I'm a WRONG NUMBER, remember???"

Well, I guess that was the wrong thing to say to Steve. There was a long silence and finally Steve said, "Kelly, I think we need to end this relationship."

"Steve, we don't have a relationship, I'm a wrong number that you've been calling for over a year. You don't know what I look like, you don't know where I live, you don't know anything about me."

"Well, regardless, I think it is time we stopped talking."

"Okay, Steve. I wish you luck, whatever you decide to do."

"Goodbye Kelly."

And he hung up. And that is how my wrong number broke up with me. I've never heard from him since. But whenever I answer the phone and someone asks for a name that isn't my own, I wonder for a millisecond if it is Steve, calling to catch me up on his life.

Just Say No

Kelly: I'm looking forward to your dinner party on Sunday. What can I bring?

Anonymous: Well, you know those muscle relaxers you have?

Kelly: Wow. Most people respond with 'a bottle of wine' or 'a dessert.' Not a drug order.

Anonymous: You asked, Kelly.

Kelly: I feel like a drug dealer.

Anonymous: My back is hurting and it is Friday and I can't see my chiropractor until next week. Help a girl out, Kelly.

Kelly: Fine, I'll bring three pills as a party favor but that is it! You have to see your doctor next week, promise?

Anonymous: I promise.

Kelly: And you know, it's a slippery slope. First you start asking me for muscle relaxers, next you're going to want to hit into my stash of Percocet.

Anonymous: You have Percocet?

Kelly: Don't even think about it.

Planning Ahead

"Patricia, it's Kelly."

"Oh boy, you only call me by my full name when something is wrong. What's going on?"

"When I die I need you to be in charge of my funeral."

"Kelly, is there something you want to tell me?"

"No, don't be silly. I'm perfectly fine. But I had a conversation with Bob last night about dying and, quite frankly, it became obvious that you'll need to handle my funeral arrangements."

"What did he say?"

"It all started when I asked him if he wanted to be buried or cremated when he died. He refused to answer me on the grounds that he would be dead, and therefore, it would not matter to him. He's such an engineer."

"What does that have to do with your funeral?"

"Because then I told him that I want to be cremated. He informed me that he plans to *stuff* me instead. And you know if he stuffs me, he's going to make my boobs even bigger than they are now. I'm going to end up looking like some weird-ass dead Dolly Parton look-alike."

"I'm not sure that's legal, Kelly. I mean the stuffing part, not the boob part."

"If it isn't, I'm sure it will be soon. Did you know you can have your ashes compressed into a diamond? Or shot out into space? Or incorporated into an artificial reef and sunk into the ocean? It's just a matter of time before you can be stuffed, too."

"Kelly, you're crazy."

"Maybe, but you are the most organized person I know, so I want you to make sure I am cremated. Also, I'll feel better if I know you'll be taking take care of my funeral.

Have a nice party afterwards. Bob will be too overcome with grief to deal with everything. I've got all the instructions written down. I'll email them to you."

"Of course you will."

"I've also drafted my obituary and selected the photograph I want you to use."

"What if you don't die for, say, another ten or twenty years? "

"Well, duh, Pat, obviously I'm going to have to keep them both updated. I'll send you a new file every so often."

"Oh, my God, I can't even believe we're having this conversation."

"Listen, about my remains; I'm leaning towards the whole diamond thing. I like the idea of being turned into a big giant rock that Bob can wear on a chain around his neck. It gives an entirely new meaning to that saying, 'Diamonds are forever,' doesn't it?"

"Kelly, I'll tell you right now that I'm only taking it as far as the cremation. I am not going to be responsible for your ashes."

"Okay, fine. But listen, I also need you to do something else."

"What else could there possibly be?"

"When I die, you need to let Bob mourn for about six months, then you need to find him a woman."

"Are you kidding me?"

"No, Pat, I'm dead serious. Heh, heh, get it? *Dead serious.* Anyway, I want to make sure Bob has someone to grow old with. And you know how men are. After about six months or so of mourning, I'm worried that he'll do something stupid and end up with some horrible witch who just wants to spend all of his retirement and then dump him for the pool boy. So I want you to get him onto one of those online dating services and find him a good woman."

"I'm not sure I want that responsibility, Kelly."

"Don't worry, I've asked Victoria to do the same thing, so you'll have help."

"Kelly, you're about the weirdest friend I've ever had."

"True, but you love me anyway, admit it."

"I love you, Kelly."

"I love you, too, Pat."

Firing Friends

Dear <name deleted to protect ~~Jarrod~~ >,

As you know, my son Gary is getting married in two months and I have agreed to host and cater this wedding at my house. I also agreed to allow my future daughter-in-law and the maid of honor to stay with us the night before the wedding and get ready in our master bedroom. And the last time I checked, I was also working full-time.

Last night, my son called me. My own flesh and blood actually said, "Mom, we need to talk. I want to make it clear that this is my wedding, not yours."

"I don't know what you're talking about, Gary."

"Mom, you are taking over the wedding. Especially the food. I do not want food I can't pronounce served at this wedding. I like simple food, Mom, good simple food."

"Gary, that email I sent with the different hors d'oeuvre ideas was just a suggestion."

"Mom, listen to me. DO NOT go all Martha Stewart on me. I'm serious."

"Okay, okay. I'll try to involve mayonnaise in as many dishes as possible, okay?"

"Fine. Now, another thing. This is a small wedding, Mom. SMALL. And personal for me and Geneva. You can tell your friends to cancel their flights right now."

"Dammit Gary."

"Mom!"

"Fine, fine. I'll tell them to cancel. But I've got to have Maggie, Ellen and...."

"Mom, calm down. I know you need your posse with you. That's fine. Just get a grip, okay?"

And so, ~~Jarrod~~, I write this letter to you having gotten a "grip" on myself. With no help from you, I might add.

I thought to myself, "Gee, I still don't have anything to wear, and I'm the mother of the groom." And of course, it would be natural for me to turn to you, my best gay friend, for help in this area. But unfortunately, you hate to shop.

Then I thought, "Well, I definitely need to do something with my hair." But I can't ask you for help with that because you don't know the first thing about fixing hair.

Then I thought, "I have to completely change the catering menu now that Gary's given me a stern talking to." But, as you well know, you hate to cook. I'm not sure you can even boil water. In fact, the last time you invited me over for a meal, I ended up cooking dinner for six people.

So, my dear ~~Jarrod~~, it has become painfully obvious to me that you are completely worthless as an official gay friend. So I'm firing you. I will continue to consider you one of my dearest, most loved, best friends until the day I die. But I am definitely going to have to recruit someone else to take on the job as my official gay friend. I hope you understand.

Love,
Kelly

P.S. Do not be late for the wedding or I will kill you.

Part Seven

Family

Mom Says
You're Adopted – Part One

One of the side benefits of being the oldest sibling in a family is that there are always more photos of you as a child than the rest of the family combined. Growing up I told my brother and sister this was because I was a much more beautiful baby, and they were both probably adopted. My sister, Lesley, who is two years younger than me, would believe me and get all upset. I'd go on to point out other proof, like her baby toe was shaped differently than mine, her eyebrows weren't pointed at the top like mine (and my father's), and general stuff like that. She was always pretty easy to bait. When I got older, I will admit that I felt a bit sorry for her, and perhaps a little ashamed of my behavior. Like the time I talked her into going to school wearing every single pair of underwear she owned. She was about five or six years old, and when she had to go potty she was in there for so long that the teacher finally went to find out what her problem was. She found my sister crying in the stall with about 14 pair of underwear all jumbled up around her thighs. Poor Lesley did not think to pull them up in order, and it was a total mess.

Then there was the time she woke up screaming in the middle of the night because of a bad dream. We shared a queen size bed, and so she woke me up too. My mother came running into the room with her hair all disheveled and her bathrobe flying behind her. I'm sure she expected to see blood all over the walls or something equally as horrible, because Lesley had a serious set of lungs. It took quite a while for my mom to calm her down. I just lay in bed next to her, annoyed that my sleep had been interrupted. When my mother got up to go back to her bedroom, I waited until her back was turned and then leaned over to Lesley. In the sweetest voice imaginable, I said, "Here Lesley, let me tuck you in, it will be all right." What my mother did not see was the huge monster face I made, complete with chomping teeth and rolling eyeballs. I shaped my hands into big monster claws and slowly descended upon my terrified sister. She tried to push herself back into the mattress, but to no avail. Her eyes widened and her face turned beet red. She was so traumatized that although her mouth was open, no sound emitted. Then slowly a howl began to emerge, coming up from the bottom of her toes, working its way through her lungs, and out of her mouth. It was unbelievable. My mother whipped around and stared at us both. Now that I'm an adult, I realize that she was thinking, "Are you fucking kidding me?"

I looked at my mother with wide eyes and the most innocent face imaginable. Artists could have used my face as their model for the Madonna. "What, what? I was just trying to tuck her in!" I exclaimed. "She's not normal." Without proof, there was really nothing Mom could do. She gathered Lesley in her arms and carried her back into the master bedroom. I rolled over to the middle of the bed and went back to sleep.

Just to set the record straight, its not like I was mean to her all the time. I was selective in my torturing and used it sparingly when she was being particularly annoying. But I'm still not sure she's ever recovered from being hog-tied, gagged, and shoved under the bed. Mom kept asking, "What is that thumping noise?" and since we lived in a townhouse, I just blamed it on the neighbors. Lesley was pretty hysterical by the time she untied herself and escaped. So, because of these incidents, as an adult, I feel a certain obligation to make things up to my sister.

This is why, for a very long time, I had the responsibility of telling Mom and Dad the bad news on behalf of Lesley. It usually started with a casual phone call from me, asking my parents to lunch. They would naively agree and then somewhere in between the salad and dessert, I would drop the bomb. Once my mother looked at me and said, "I don't know why I keep falling for this, Kelly. You keep inviting me for lunch, and I keep saying yes like a fool. This has to stop!"

And so it came that one day many years ago, Lesley asked me to come have lunch with her. Given the track record for lunches in our family, I was immediately suspicious. "Why, what is wrong?" I asked.

"I just need to talk to you, Kelly," she replied.

"Okay, but if anyone is dying you would tell me right away, right?"

"Nobody is dying. For crying out loud, just meet me for lunch."

I met Lesley for lunch and we both immediately ordered a glass of wine. Clearly this was going to be something big. I stared at Lesley while she fidgeted with her drink, her napkin, and her keys. She lit up a cigarette and then dropped the lighter. Finally I couldn't take it anymore. Staring intently into her face, I began my interrogation.

"Nobody is dying, right?"

"Everybody is fine, I swear."

"So, this is about you, right?"

"Yes."

"And the kids are okay, right?"

"Yes."

"So it must be you. Oh, my God, your marriage is in trouble, right?"

"Yes."

"Are you leaving Dave?"

"Yes."

"Are you sure there is no way it's going to work?"

"Yes."

"How do you know for sure?"

"I'm gay."

"Holy shit."

"Yes, holy shit."

"I love you, Lesley."

"I love you, too, Kelly."

And that is how I found out my sister was gay. Never, in my entire life, had it ever crossed my mind that this was a possibility. With the exception of my occasional torturing, she had as normal a childhood as anyone else. She dated, graduated from high school, got married, and produced three wonderful daughters. She had been a faithful wife for 20 years. She is one of the best mothers I have ever known. But I know my sister, so this was not a passing phase. This was a major life moment and decisions had to be made.

"Have you told Mom and Dad?" I asked.

"No."

Then she sat there and stared at me from across the table.

"Holy shit, Lesley. There is no way I'm telling them this one. You can forget it!"

"Kelly, come on. Just take them out to lunch."

"Lesley, first of all, I am pretty sure Mom is on to the whole lunch strategy. Second, this is like major, major big news. You have to tell them yourself. I will go with you and support you, but this has to come from you, not me!"

A few days later, Lesley and I sat on the front porch swing at my parent's house. I held her hand as worked up her courage to share the big news.

"Mom and Dad, I need you to know that Dave and I have separated," announced Lesley. "I've moved into a townhouse."

"Oh, my God," exclaimed Mom.

Dad sat quietly and took in the scene. After a moment of silence my mom asked Lesley if she was okay, and how things were with Dave and the girls. Lesley explained that she and the girls were fine and the separation was happening rather amicably.

"Dave is being a total hero about all this," I told my parents. "He understands that it is a final decision and he's dealing with everything incredibly well."

Of course, there was further discussion about where Lesley was living now, what she was going to be doing for income, how the girls were handling everything, and the typical type of Q&A you get when you announce the end of a 20-year marriage.

Once Mom and Dad had been given some time to absorb that little bit of news, it was time to drop the other bomb.

"Are you doing okay?" asked Lesley. "Because there is more."

Lesley started squeezing my hand tightly as we swung back and forth. "Just say it," I whispered in her ear. "Just say it now."

"What, what?" asked Mom.

It was at this point that Dad started giggling. This was a somewhat unexpected reaction. Lesley looked at him and said, "I'm glad you're taking this so well, Dad."

He laughed some more. "Well, I know what's coming," he said. Then he gestured at Mom with his thumb. "But she doesn't have a clue."

"What, what?" asked Mom again.

"Just say it, just say it!" I hissed at Lesley.

"I'm GAY!" declared Lesley.

"And that is why Dave is acting like he just got out of prison," I howled.

Lesley turned to me and punched my arm. My Dad grabbed his sides and laughed some more. And my Mother looked at all of us and asked, "Is it too early for wine?"

I couldn't think of a better reason to drink wine at 11 a.m. so I immediately got glasses for everyone. As we sipped Merlot, my parents and Lesley had a long talk about her life and what the future might hold. Most importantly, they assured Lesley that their love and respect for her remained unshaken. They also made it clear that after 20 years, Dave was a member of our family and would remain so for as long as he chose.

Later, when Lesley questioned my Dad about his reaction, he really couldn't say why he wasn't surprised. Nor was my brother surprised when he eventually found out. Like me, prior to her announcement it had never occurred to either of them to question her preference on the matter. But once it was said out loud, everything just clicked, and each of us in the family thought to ourselves, "Of course, that makes so much sense." Then we just moved on with our lives.

I realize that for many, this type of news would have blown the family apart. I am fortunate to have been raised by the two amazing people that are my parents. And the truth is, I don't really care where I rank in the birth order of this family. I just thank God every day that I am a member.

Mom Says
You're Adopted – Part Two

I was six years old when my brother, Dan, was born. I don't remember being too impressed when he showed up. He just took up space and my parents' attention. Plus, there didn't seem to be much of a win in it for me. So I ignored him and concentrated on more important matters, like decorating my bike for the annual Easter parade and torturing Lesley.

Things changed when he got a little older and you could actually interact with him. Looking back, I realize he was a very cute kid. He was roly-poly in all the right places and he walked around like a little old man, with his hands clasped behind his back. He reminded you of an absent-minded professor because he was always thinking and observing. His dark brown eyes, the color of a deeply roasted coffee bean, missed nothing. Just when you thought you were dealing with a regular little boy, he'd look at you and ask, "When you're dreaming, can you dream that you're having a dream?" and you'd be left there staring at him and wondering, "Who the hell are you, kid?"

He was also incredibly confident. I would try the old, "Mom says you're adopted," routine and he would just stare at me with these wise, four-year-old eyes and smile. He wasn't buying it for one minute. Then he would go outside, round up all the little girls in the neighborhood, and charge them five cents apiece to see his penis. My brother came out of the birth canal figuring out how to make money.

I think when Dan was born, the Universe, or God, or whoever is in charge of this sort of thing, realized they couldn't just give Dan this incredible intelligence, confidence, and entrepreneurial spirit, (not to mention perfectly straight white teeth) without making him work for it. So in order to make it interesting, someone up there said, "Let's spend the first ten years of his life trying to kill him. If he makes it through the first decade, we'll stop messing with him."

I am not exaggerating. By the time he entered his eleventh year, my brother had nearly drowned so many times that we lost count. He fell, head first, from a three-story banister onto a marble floor. He spent several days in the hospital — the doctors could not believe he wasn't in a coma. He narrowly escaped abduction from a taxi by a wild-eyed, West-African militant. Finally, he nearly fell out of a car going 60 miles per hour when he opened the passenger door to "see what would happen." My father, who was driving the car, grabbed my brother's shirt collar and pulled him back to safety just as Dan was pitching head first onto the asphalt. That was the day I learned several choice curse words, courtesy of my father's younger days in the Navy.

When Dan was four years old, he stopped walking and began to run everywhere. He did not stop running until he turned twelve, which is the year we learned about the correlation between sugar and ADHD. Unfortunately, his fat little legs often kept going long after his brain told them to stop. As a result, he has several scars on his forehead, courtesy of any number of doors, wall corners, and the occasional piece of furniture. It got so bad that one morning as I was primping in the bathroom and my brother was running through the house, I heard a loud "splat," followed by a sickening, crunchy sort of "thump." The nanny assigned to watch my brother at all times started yelling for help. I didn't even bother going out to the kitchen. I knew what I would see: my brother splayed on the floor, with his eyes rolled back into his head and blood pouring all over the place from yet another split in his forehead while his nanny hysterically tried to revive him before my parents got home from work.

Because of this penchant for self-destruction, the entire family took to indulging my brother whenever possible. Who knew how much longer we'd have him around? So Dan grew up hearing the word "no" a lot less than most kids. I don't mean in a spoiled, you-never-get-in-trouble, kind of way. He got in trouble all the time. Seriously, *all the time.* I'm talking about allowing the kid to follow his interests, wherever they might take him. And for Dan, those interests involved starting businesses.

The first time we took him to the library, around age five, he was so enthralled by the concept that he came home and glued envelopes to the back of every book in the house. Lesley and I had to check out books approximately fourteen times a day for two weeks. Dan was always claiming that our books were past due, thus requiring that we pay a fine of five cents per book. Lesley and I just took the money from the pile of change on my dad's dresser and gave it to my brother. We knew he'd lose it in about ten minutes and then we could go put it back.

The first Sunday after attending church (instead of getting dumped in the kiddy room), my brother came home and rearranged the living room. He placed all the dining room chairs in rows down the middle and put on my father's long brown bathrobe. It had a hood, which he placed over his little round head. The rest of the family had to attend mass every day for about a week. Dan would stand in front of the stereo with the coffee table as a makeshift altar.

He would hold open the Bible and begin to pray. Unfortunately, he could not read yet, nor could he remember what the priest said during the sermon, so he made it up as he went along. "We are gathered here for praying," Dan would intone, "and for the bread of the mighty and the angels in heaven and God Bless America!" Then, naturally, we had to pass around the donation basket and give him all our change. In defense of Dan's avariciousness, he also loved the part when it was time to show each other the sign of peace. "Everyone hugs now," he would yell as he counted up his change. "Lots of hugging, please!"

When he was six years old we moved to Greece. We lived in a suburb near Athens, and on just about every corner, there were little shacks called "kiosks" that sold newspapers, fruit, candy, and any number of convenience items. Dan was in heaven. Commandeering one of the large shipping boxes from our move, he spent an entire day cutting out windows and a door and coloring the outside of the box to look like a kiosk. He then walked over to the local stores and talked them into giving him fruit on consignment to sell in his shop. How he managed to pull this off is a mystery. I can picture him now, this serious, three-and-a-half foot tall entrepreneur negotiating oranges and apples with the bemused shop owners. For several weeks, every time you found something small missing from your room, the first place you would look was Dan's store. Naturally, he was always more than happy to sell our property back to us.

By the time he was ten, we were living in the States. Now that Dan no longer had a language barrier to deal with, plus access to a telephone and phone book, there was no stopping him. Every day was an adventure for my parents, as Dan still relied on them for transportation. He decided to become a magician, practicing his magic tricks on all of us until we were struck dumb from exhaustion. One Sunday, he announced to my father that he needed to be driven to a local church, as he had been hired to perform his magic tricks at a function there. Imagine the Pastor's surprise when "Dan the Magnificent" turned out to be a chubby ten-year-old boy wearing a top hat and oversized cape, strolling in with the confidence of David Copperfield. Mom put the kibosh on Dan's career when she intercepted a call from the local telephone company. They were just calling to confirm the half-page advertisement he had recently ordered.

Having made some money from his short-lived career as a magician, Dan decided he needed to secure his own transportation. I think this had something to do with the threats he'd received from my parents about the consequences of any more last-minute scrambles to get him somewhere. Plus he'd just learned about paper routes. Driving home from a shopping trip, my parents were alarmed to see a small boy riding a bicycle through the middle of traffic. Oblivious to the blaring horns and narrowly missed bumpers, the kid furiously peddled his way in between a large van and the local bus. The closer my parents got to the boy, the more familiar he appeared. "Oh, my God," exclaimed my mother, "I think that's Daniel!"

Sure enough, it was. My brother had read about a bike for sale in the local classifieds. He grabbed his wallet and walked for several miles across town to negotiate the purchase of his new two-wheeler. He was on his way back to the house when he was intercepted by my parents. Throwing the bike into the trunk and strapping my brother into the back seat, they drove home to fix themselves each a very strong martini.

Desperate to find something that would keep my brother closer to home, my parents bought him a CB Radio. *Smokey and the Bandit* was Dan's favorite movie at the time, so he was delighted to spend most of his waking hours sitting in his bedroom chatting with truckers all over the state. It didn't take him long to pick up the their unique vernacular. It became common to walk by Dan's bedroom and hear, "Breaker, breaker, this is Station 139. I've got a Smokey report — there's a bear in a plain brown wrapper waiting up in the bush at mile-marker 44. You probably want to back it on down." While this was annoying, at least my parents could keep an eye on him.

I'm sure the CB Radio station idea would have worked for a much longer time, had my mother not woken up one morning at six a.m. to find a big, burly, middle-aged truck driver wearing overalls and a three-day beard standing in the upstairs hallway. He and my eleven-year-old brother were discussing the pros and cons of Dan's base station. Apparently Dan had started a conversation with this man around five a.m. and invited him over to the house for a cup of coffee and to "talk shop." It took my mom several hours to calm down, even though the truck driver was very polite and left immediately after seeing the look on my mother's face.

To this day, if you bring this incident up to my mom, she will tell you that she's blocked it from her memory. She chooses, instead, to talk about how later in the day when the mail was delivered, Dan received a letter from the White House. President Carter, while sincerely appreciating the kind invitation to supper, regretfully declined due to several pressing matters of State.

Clarence

I don't think you automatically like your brother or sister when they arrive. Let's face it — all they do is crap, cry and suck the life force from your parents for the first few months, while you're left wondering when you stopped being the center of the universe. Sure, you automatically love them because everyone says you have to, but it takes time to establish the bonds that turn you both into friends as well. This happens at different stages for everyone. For my brother and me, it happened when he was in sixth grade.

My mother was a secretary in a law office when I was eighteen. She called me from work one morning. "Kelly, I need you to go down to the middle school and find out what is going on with your brother," she said. "He is in the principal's office. It has something to do with a snake in his pocket that he refuses to turn over to the teacher. I simply cannot leave work right now, nor am I sure I can deal with a snake."

I drove to the school and went to the office. Sure enough, there was Dan sitting in a chair in the lobby. He was extremely indignant. Apparently, he had found a garter snake on the way to school. Delighted with his new friend, whom he immediately named "Clarence," he put the snake in his coat pocket for safekeeping. He had a vague plan of building a wonderful home for Clarence in his bedroom while he figured out how to make money as a snake charmer.

Unfortunately, Clarence crawled out of Dan's pocket at one point during the morning, bringing the entire sixth grade class to a screeching halt. Girls at that age need little encouragement to start squealing and screaming. Once they get going, it is not unlike the sound of a large group of cornered hyenas. Dan's teacher demanded that Clarence be released outside. Dan refused. Dan was then marched into the Principal's office. The principal demanded that he release Clarence outside. Dan refused once again. He simply was not going to give up his new best friend. At their wits' end, the school staff called my mother and requested that she come pick up Dan (and Clarence) immediately.

Walking with Dan back to my car, I impatiently asked him why he wouldn't give up the stupid snake. "Because he is my friend!" he exclaimed. "I can make him happy."

I looked at him standing there, as disheveled and sweaty as only a sixth grade boy can appear. His shirt was hanging half out of his pants and his right shoe was untied. His brown hair, cut into an unfortunate bowl-shaped style, kept sweeping into his eyes. He impatiently brushed it away with chubby, grubby fingers and then reached into his coat pocket to make sure Clarence was still in place.

My heart melted.

Getting into the car, Dan and I drove around town for a very long time. We talked about life and the roles that people, animals, and reptiles played in it. We talked about friendship, and how sometimes doing the right thing for your friends wasn't always the same as doing what would make you happy.

Eventually, we stopped at a field by the house. It was close to where Dan had met Clarence earlier that day. I stood back as Dan walked into the tall brown grass. Slowly he took Clarence out of his pocket. Giving him one more long, gentle stroke down his shiny scales, Dan let his friend go free. Then he turned and with a sigh, walked back over to the car. I put my arms around him and hugged him close. His head fit right under my chin and he smelled like shampoo and sweat and dirt, with a little bit of peanut butter thrown in for good measure. "You did the right thing," I whispered in his ear. "I'm proud of you."

It has been thirty-four years since the day we set Clarence free. Dan doesn't fit under my chin any longer, and he has long since lost his baby fat. He is a successful entrepreneur. He is as inquisitive and curious today as he was in his youth. But sometimes, when he is standing across the room, if I squint my eyes, I can still see the lonely little boy who just wanted to have a new friend. And my heart melts all over again.

Thanksgiving

Dear Friends,

I hope everyone enjoyed Thanksgiving and that it was somewhat less dangerous than mine. Normally when the dinner is going to be at my house, I assign everyone a dish except for my bachelor brother, who is put in charge of bringing celery salt. This year, since I now have seven bottles of the stuff (does it ever go bad?), I told Dan to bring green beans instead. Seriously, how can you screw up green beans?

This year there were only ten of us for dinner at my house. Everyone arrived around 2:00 p.m. The plan was to eat around 3:30. In addition to a host of wonderful dishes, I made sure we had two types of stuffing because one needed to be meatless. I made this just for my brother, the vegetarian, who was late.

He called to apologize, saying since he still had to buy the ingredients at the store he would not arrive until about 2:30. I told him not to worry, he would still have time to prepare his beans before we sat down for supper.

At 3:00 I had my mother call him to find out where he was.

At 3:30 he showed up with all the supplies, full of apologies.

Then he said, "This will only take about 40 minutes."

I just stared at him and blinked.

So with every other dish warming in the oven and the turkey sitting covered in tin foil, we swung into action.

I asked my parents to clean the green beans because my brother didn't even have the foresight to buy pre-cleaned beans. With the bean-cleaning project well underway, my brother started chopping the onions. While he was bragging about his new and extremely expensive professional chef's knife, he cut his thumb and bled all over the chopping board. Exasperated, I grabbed my inexpensive, not professional, and somewhat dull chopping knife, took over with a fresh board and a new onion. I promptly cut my finger and bled all over the board, the floor, the drawer, the onion, and the kitchen counter. I'm surprised it didn't hit the ceiling.

"Mom," I said very calmly as I wrapped my finger in a kitchen towel. "Could you please wipe up my blood?"

"Of course, dear," she replied. "I'd be happy to." She then turned to my Dad and said, "Jack, you're on your own with the beans."

"I've always wondered what it felt like to be a sous chef," said Dad.

I made Bob inspect my finger because I wanted him to feel sorry for me. After much discussion between Bob, Uncle Jim, and my dad, it was determined that I did not need stitches — a good firm compress would be fine. So Bob found the medical kit and wrapped my finger with two Band-Aids and gave me a stern lecture about being more careful in the future. I then jumped back into action.

The beans were completed in 30 minutes. Everyone helped bring the food to the dining room table, which was beautifully decorated with gourds, fall flowers, and candles. Two of my grandchildren were there, running around and charming everyone. We all joined hands while my dad said Grace, thanking the Lord that I had not killed my brother.

My mother commented later that she was amazed at how calm I was during the entire afternoon. The truth is that in the grand scheme of things, I felt so grateful to be surrounded by people I love, with my grandchildren running under foot, and with my husband completely oblivious to all the commotion while watching football and teaching my grandson, Eli, a new wrestling slam every time he passed by, that I found myself full of grace and gratitude.

The holiday is now over and we have all jumped back into work. As we look towards Christmas and Hanukkah, here is what I wish for all of you: that each day you take a moment to fill yourselves with grace and gratitude for what you have, the people you love and those that love you in return, just as I love all of you.

Happy Holidays!

Love,

Kelly

You Can't Make
This Sh*t Up – Part One

"Lesley, it's me. I need you to put on your doctor's hat."

"Kelly, I'm a nurse, not a doctor."

"Whatever. Anyway, I was just curious. What are the symptoms of a concussion?"

"What do you mean, curious? What have you done now?"

"Why do you assume it's me?"

"Because I'm your sister, that's why."

"Yeah, I guess you know me too well. Anyway, I think I have a concussion."

"Why?"

"A 300-pound man fell on me in a bar."

"Holy cow, Kelly. Are you serious?"

"Lesley, I can't make this shit up. I don't actually remember it happening, but Lucy from my office called me after I flew back from Orlando to ask me how I was feeling. I told her that I had bruises all over my body and a big knot on my head, but I couldn't remember how it happened. That's when she told me about the guy falling on top of me."

"So this happened in Orlando?"

"Yes, two days ago. I was there on business and a bunch of us went to a bar after dinner. I asked a co-worker to dance and pulled on his arm. I guess I took him by surprise because he lost his balance and fell on me."

"What happened then?"

"Well, apparently I was pretty loopy. Lucy and Danielle thought I was just drunk so they took me back to the hotel and put me to bed. When I woke up, I couldn't remember how I got back to the hotel room. Then I went to the airport and flew home."

"Congratulations, Kelly. You've managed to do every single possible thing you are not supposed to do with a concussion. You NEVER let someone go to sleep after a concussion. You do NOT leave them alone and you CERTAINLY do not let them get on an airplane the very next day. I swear to God, I'm driving up to your office in Connecticut and giving everyone a first aid lesson!"

"Well, Lesley, in defense of Lucy and Danielle, I had been drinking. I can see where they could have thought that I was just very drunk."

"Kelly, a 300-pound man fell on you. What more do you want?"

"Okay, just calm down. I see your point. Don't worry, though. I have an appointment with my doctor this afternoon. I'll let you know what happens."

"Fine, but you better call me back — or else."

"I will, I promise. Just don't tell Mom, okay?"

This goes to show that no matter how old you and your siblings are, any maturity you've gained over the years can fly out of the window in a millisecond. All it takes is a "Don't tell Mom," and a "Call me back or else," and you are both back in elementary school.

The doctor confirmed that I had a mild concussion. He said one of the signs of a concussion is amnesia, and that was why I could not remember the incident.

I called my sister to give her the update.

"I definitely have a concussion."

"This is what you get for getting drunk in a bar, Kelly."

"Actually, the doctor said that it was a good thing I was drunk. It made me fall loosely. If I had been sober I would have stiffened up and probably broken a bone or something."

"So what are you saying?"

"I'm saying that when you go to a bar, you should probably get drunk because you never know when a 300-pound man is going to fall on you. That's what I'm saying."

"Kelly, you're crazy."

"Maybe, but I probably just saved your life with that bit of advice."

You Can't Make
This Sh*t Up – Part Two

"Lesley, it's me. I went by the hospital and visited Mom today. She looks a lot better."

"Oh, good. The Doctor said she might go home tomorrow, provided her oxygen level gets a little higher. Pneumonia is nothing to play around with."

"No kidding. Do you know what Dad told me? Apparently Mom didn't want him to call an ambulance so he rolled her out to the car on her sewing chair. Can you imagine the scene? Why wouldn't they call an ambulance?"

"Who knows, Kelly? When Dad called me Monday night and described Mom's symptoms, I told him he needed to get her to the hospital right away."

"Well, it's a good thing Doctor Watterson was available to take their call."

"Very funny, Kelly. I'm a nurse, not a doctor, but anyone would have told them to go to the emergency room. She was pretty sick. Anyway, how are you doing? Are you recovering from your concussion? How long has it been? Three weeks?"

"Yes, three weeks tomorrow. Funny you should ask. I got rear-ended today while I was sitting at a red light. My chin hit the steering wheel and now I have the Honda logo on my face."

"Oh my God, Kelly! You mean to tell me you sustained yet another head injury?"

"Chill out, Lesley. I hit my chin, not my head."

"And what do you think your chin is attached to, Kelly? What…is…your…chin…attached…to?"

"Huh. I hadn't really looked at it that way."

"I'm sure you didn't, Kelly. This family is falling apart. Do you know how dangerous it is to sustain a head injury after a concussion? Do you? Do you?"

"Lesley, stop yelling at me. I am the victim here, remember? I am the one walking around with the Honda logo on her face."

"Tell me what happened."

"I was sitting at a red light finishing up a phone conversation with Jarrod when I heard a large crash. 'Wow, someone just got hit,' I thought.

"Then I heard another bang, except this time my chin hit the middle of my steering wheel and then my head snapped back to hit my seat. It was so fast that it was over before I realized what had happened."

"Oh God. What happened to the guy who hit you? Was he hurt?"

"Well, it was a double car accident. A guy driving a very large white delivery truck hit a big black SUV and the SUV hit me."

"Wow."

"Oh, it gets better. The guy who hit me was a police officer driving a county-owned vehicle."

"You're kidding!"

"Nope. So regardless of what happened to me, at least I'm not the poor fool who hit a cop! Anyway, right after the accident, the two other drivers and I just sat in our cars for a moment. I was holding my chin because it hurt like hell. Finally I got out of my car and walked towards the guy behind me to ask if he was okay. He said, 'I'm fine, but you're bleeding.'

"When I pulled my hand away and saw the blood I went all girlie on the guy. My knees got weak, and he had to hold my hand, and then I was crying just a little bit.

He kept assuring me it was a very small cut and hardly bleeding."

"Did you tell him you'd had a concussion?"

"Yes, Lesley, of course I told him. I was worried because I figured it might mess me up some more. So he called the ambulance and before I knew it, I had medics, firemen, and policemen hovering all around me.

"One of the medics walked over to assess my injuries and asked me if I was okay. 'I'm fine,' I said. 'I'm just worried because I got a concussion three weeks ago and I'm afraid this accident might have made it worse.' Then the medic asked me how I got the concussion."

"Oh, my God, what did you tell him?"

"I told him the truth — that a 300 pound man fell on me in a bar. The medic just stared at me and blinked. 'Are you serious?' he asked."

"So I said, 'Look, I can't make this shit up.'"

"He probably thought you were a nut case."

"No doubt. So I figured I would call and tell you about my latest adventure so you could worry about me."

"Very funny, Kelly."

"Also, don't tell Mom, okay? She has enough to worry about."

"I won't tell her as long as you stay with someone tonight in case you go into a coma or something."

"Lesley, I can't believe you are blackmailing me. I'm 50 years old. Aren't we past the blackmail stage?"

"No, we are not. I know Bob is out of town and you are alone. You either stay with a friend tonight or else."

"Fine, I'll stay with Maggie, okay?"

"Fine. And I want to talk to Maggie once you get there. I need to give her instructions on what to look for tonight."

"Okay. But don't start using a lot of long nurse words and medical terminology. You know how you get when you are talking about stuff like this."

"I'll keep it plain English. You just make sure she calls me."

"Okay, but I think you are forgetting that I'm the victim here, Lesley."

"You either do what I say or you WILL be a victim, I promise you that!"

"I love you, Lesley."

"I love you too, Kelly. So don't make me hurt you."

A Conversation You Never Thought You'd Have With Your Mother

"Hey Mom, what did you do today?"

"I went with some friends to a quilt show, then we went to the fabric store."

"Did you find any good fabrics?"

"Yes. While my friends and I were there, a man came in with his wife and everyone in the store noticed that he was wearing a gun under his jacket. They were all staring at him and looking worried. He must have noticed because he started to reach for his back pocket. All the girls got very nervous, but of course, I knew what he was doing. He just pulled out his wallet and showed everyone his license to carry a concealed weapon."

"Wow, that must have been a little nerve wracking."

"Well, you know what I did then."

"Oh God, Mom, you didn't."

"Yes, I did. I took MY wallet out and showed him MY license to carry a concealed weapon."

"Lord, I thought you were going to tell me you whipped out your gun."

"Kelly, don't be ridiculous, I wouldn't pull out a gun. I just didn't want him to think he was the only person in the quilt store with a license to carry a concealed weapon."

"Good grief, a show down at the quilt store. What's next, Mom?"

"Don't get smart with me Kelly, I'm still your mother."

"Mom, you know this conversation is going in my book, right?"

The Greatest Party Ever

My parents recently celebrated their 50th wedding anniversary at an historic inn located somewhere in the Virginia countryside. (Shortly you will understand why I cannot reveal the exact location.) I announced that I would take charge of the decorations, despite the fact that I was traveling on business for the two weeks prior to the event.

Four days before the party, I remembered how much my mother loves hydrangeas. Since I was working in Connecticut that week, I decided to delegate this task to my younger sister.

"Lesley, I need you to get me some hydrangeas."

"What's a hydrangea?"

"Good grief, Lesley, everyone knows what a hydrangea is. Those big fluffy balls of blue and pink flowers in the big bushes are everywhere. Do you have any?"

"I don't have any, but I think my neighbor has a bush of them."

"Well, I need a dozen."

"I don't know him that well, Kelly. I'm not going to go ask for a dozen hydrangeas from his garden."

"Well, then wait until it's dark and go steal them."

"Don't you think he'll notice when he's missing a dozen flowers off his bush?"

"Just space out where you cut them off and he'll probably never notice."

"Kelly, I'm not stealing hydrangeas for you."

"Well, then go find a friend who has a hydrangea bush. Grab a dozen flowers and call me when you're done."

"Why don't you do it?"

"Because, Lesley, I'm up here in Connecticut. I don't

get home until Friday afternoon, the night before the party. I wish I could bring them home with me because you can't swing a dead cat up here without hitting a hydrangea bush. But TSA won't let me take a dozen of those puppies on the plane so you have to do this."

"Well, I'll look around and try to find some for you, but I really think you're starting to lose it, Kelly."

Two days later, I called my sister to find out how she was doing with her mission.

"Kelly, nobody I know has a rhododendron bush."

"Ohfortheloveofgod, Lesley. I said *hydrangea*, not rhododendron."

"Well, I can't find those either."

"Just call Mom and Dad and find out how everything else is going for the party. Do you think you can do that?"

"Yes, but I'm telling you, Kelly, I think you're losing it."

I was supposed to fly home Friday afternoon, but summer storms kept everyone grounded. I called my sister to give her the good news.

"Lesley, we may have a problem. I'm stuck in Connecticut."

"Oh, dear."

"Oh, dear is right, Lesley. If this weather grounds all the flights, I'll have to drive home, which means I won't get there until tomorrow morning. So I may need you to go set up everything at the inn for the party tomorrow night."

"This is all because you hate me, right?"

"Don't be ridiculous. Listen, better not tell Mom I'm still in Connecticut."

"Fine, but *get home.*"

Fortunately, the storms passed and I was home by 10:30 Friday night. On the plus side, sitting in the airport gave me plenty of time to put the finishing touches on the video I was creating from old family photographs. Saturday morning I got up, collected all my supplies, and went to decorate the party room at the inn. (I broke down and bought the damn hydrangeas.) Three hours before the party I realized that I did not have the extremely important dongle cord necessary to connect my Mac laptop to the television in order to show the video I'd created. I went into a panic and called Best Buy.

"Hi, this is Jeff, how can I help you?"

"Jeff, I am in the middle of a crisis. I have a Mac laptop and I have to connect it to a television in three hours to show a video at my parents 50th wedding anniversary and I don't have the connector thing."

"Do you know what type of laptop you have?"

"It's a Mac."

"Ma'am, do you know the model?"

"No, Jeff, I do not. But I can tell you it is small, silver, and missing the connector thing."

"Do you need an HGDY connector, a GHYG connector or a LMNOP connector?"

"Jeff, I know you think you're speaking English, but I have no idea what you're saying. Can you just go ask someone to pull the cable I need?"

"Please hold."

A few moments later Jeff came back on the phone.

"Ma'am, we have your connector."

"Fantastic, what's your name again?"

"Jeff."

"Now listen, Jeff. I'm going to be sending my sister over to pick up the connector. Her name is Lesley. She's short with blonde hair and she'll be asking for you. She'll probably look very pissed off when she shows up but just ignore that part."

"Uhhh."

"Jeff, do not leave the store until my sister arrives, got it?"

"Yes ma'am."

I then sent a text to my sister.

TXT: Lesley, I need you to go to Best Buy on your way here.

TXT: Are you KIDDING me???? Do you know what I have to get done before the party?

TXT: No I'm not kidding and I don't care. You have to go there and ask for a guy named Jeff and he will give you a dongle cord connector thing that you have to bring to the party. Or we can't watch the video I spent hundreds of hours creating.

TXT: Okay, fine. We'll get the dongle.

TXT: Remember to ask for Jeff. If you go around asking anyone else for a dongle you'll only embarrass yourself.

I went upstairs to freshen up and was back downstairs by 5:00 p.m. My brother showed up fifteen minutes later, miraculously on time and looking very handsome. My sister came dashing in with the much-anticipated dongle. Donnie, the family DJ, got the music playing. The flowers were perfect. When my parents arrived, I asked my mom why she was wearing dark sunglasses. A bug had bitten her face and the entire left side was swollen, so she kept her glasses on all night. She looked a little like Roy Orbison, but in a very happy way. All of a sudden all 25 people were present and accounted for! I poured myself a glass of wine and went to give my sister a very big hug.

We partied and danced all night long. We sang Karaoke, and my brother brought the house down. At midnight the innkeeper announced last call. My parents got a ride home with some of the older relatives. One of the staff hugged my sister and me, saying through her tears that we were the best family she'd ever met. The rest of us migrated to the front porch of the inn where we sat, talking, laughing, and drinking until around two in the morning.

The next day when we all woke up, most of us were still drunk. Luckily my husband had shown a modicum of restraint, so he drove us to my parents' house. That is when I realized we'd forgotten my brother back at the hotel. I called him in a panic.

"Dan, this is Kelly. We forgot you! Are you still at the hotel?"

"Oh, my God, Kelly. I think I'm still drunk!"

"We all are, it was a hell of a party. But listen — you have to get out of that hotel. The innkeeper is furious with us. I came down this morning, and when she looked at me I expected her head to start spinning around while she hissed 'get ouuuuuutt, geeettttt ouuuuutttt.'"

"Why is she pissed at us?"

"She thought we'd all be gone by ten at the latest last night."

"Are you kidding me? Doesn't she know we're Irish?"

"You know how it is. Mom and Dad went down there to book the party room looking all innocent, just a couple of helpless 73-year-olds. She had no idea what she was getting into."

"Wow, when did the party end?"

"Well, the innkeeper announced last call at midnight, which is when I walked up to the bar and said, 'In that case, give me a bottle of Chardonnay and a straw.' She didn't look too pleased."

"Oh, my God."

"Yeah, it got worse when Bob told her, 'She isn't kidding' and they had to go find a straw long enough to reach the bottom of the wine bottle. By the way, Mom wants to know where you disappeared to last night. She said she was talking to you and you got a funny look on your face and just walked away."

"She said to me, 'Dan, I don't think I've ever seen you this drunk.'"

"Were you that drunk?"

"Kelly, I couldn't even form words at that point. I had a really witty comeback for Mom, but my lips wouldn't move. So I went to bed."

"Good grief, Dan."

"Yeah, tell Mom that what I wanted to say was, 'Sure you've seen me this drunk, Mom. Remember that one time right before you sent me to military school?'"

"Heh, good one. But listen, I'm serious. You have to get out of that room. Come over here right away. That innkeeper is a woman on the edge. Save yourself while you can."

After hanging up on my brother, the rest of us sat around and reminisced about the perfect party. We kept laughing and telling stories. In the end, thanks to the wonderful people I get to call my family, and despite my Type-A personality, it was a wonderful, memorable, magical evening. And, I am happy to say, Dan did make it out alive.

How Close Can
Two People Be?

When I was 25, I watched my parents dance together. It wasn't the first time I had seen them dance, but it was the first time I paid attention. They moved together as a single unit across the floor. My father held my mother as lightly as a feather, and she smiled and swayed in his arms as though her feet were hovering above the floor. Without a word, they swung apart and back together again, knees lightly touching here, a hand on a shoulder there. For a few minutes, everyone else in the room disappeared, and I saw them alone as they moved to the music. They were lost in their private world, where nothing existed except the two of them. I realized then, as I do now, that my parents put each other ahead of everything else in their lives.

How close can two people be? They can become so integrated with each other that one begins breathing where the other leaves off. Where a single look across a room, a sigh, a touch, carries more words than a novel. They can become so connected that even when separated by continents and oceans, one person can suddenly sit up and know that at that very moment, the other is thinking of them.

It doesn't come easily or quickly. It takes time to get to the point where one person finishes the other's sentence. Where you can dance with your partner and move as one. But if you commit your life to someone else, then you have years to work on it. The two of you will see each other at your weakest, most selfish, most horrible state. You will laugh together, scream at each other, and cry in each other's arms. You'll say things you regret having ever said out loud, or things that you regret you didn't say sooner. There will be times when you look at your partner and wonder what on earth you were thinking when you said "I do." These moments may last for months. But then one day you will wake up, look at your partner, and the thought of not having this person in your life will make you lose your breath.

It takes great courage to show someone else what is inside of you. To not be afraid to be vulnerable, and to trust your partner to love you as you really are, not as others perceive you. But once you've done that with each other, then it begins. Slowly, painfully sometimes, and joyfully at other times, you will begin to meld into each other. Then one day, years from now, you will find yourselves swaying to music, real or imagined, held together with invisible strands of a lifetime of shared experience. When that time comes, look into your heart. Whatever is in there, don't be afraid to say it out loud.

A Note About The Author

Kelly Harman was born in Asmara, Ethiopia in 1962 and has walked the road less traveled ever since. She spent her childhood overseas, living in eight different countries before she came to the U.S. at the age of 16. This experience inspired an adventurous streak and disregard for convention which has yielded a rich life, overflowing with great story material.

Her experiences range from celebrating her ninth birthday at India's Taj Mahal to being evacuated with her family in the midst of a civil war in East Pakistan, from single motherhood to serial entrepreneur, and from Burning Man devotee to self-made marketing maven. Most recently Kelly came full circle back to the continent of her birthplace, celebrating her 50th birthday at the summit of Mt. Kilimanjaro.

Kelly lives in Manassas, Virginia with Bob, her husband and true love of 23 years. When she isn't writing about her adventures, Kelly loves spending time with her friends and family, but especially with her three grandchildren, teaching them the value of reckless honesty and unhindered fun.

Made in the USA
Charleston, SC
18 July 2013